TABLE OF CONTENTS

LIST OF ILLUSTRATIONS

CHAPTER I

INTRODUCTION

The Bush Administration's National Security Strategy (NSS) of September 2002, in much controversy, embraced a preemptive strategy to eliminate the threats to the United States. In addition to these preemptive measures, the NSS stated that, if necessary, the United States would act unilaterally to ensure its safety. The United States acted on both of these principles during Operation Iraqi Freedom. Although this monograph does not address the controversial nature of the NSS, it does look at the impact that these ideas may have on the U.S. Army particularly in the area of belligerent occupation. Additionally, it must be acknowledged that in the current state of world affairs, and with the current NSS, another occupation in the near future is not out of the question.

The challenge of such occupations is the military's need to reach the government's strategic aim while sustaining and protecting the military force. Successful termination of Operation Iraqi Freedom now depends not on the combat operations, but on how well the United States and the U.S. Army, in particular, reestablishes the Iraqi government and facilitates the building of a stable nation. Arguably, the United States has not performed a mission of belligerent occupation of this magnitude since the aftermath of World War II. Certainly, it is too soon to assess how well the United States has performed this mission, but an evaluation of U.S. Army doctrine on occupation is necessary due to the possible reoccurrence of this mission in the near future. This monograph examines how well current U.S. Army doctrine addresses the mission of belligerent occupation and offers recommendations.

This monograph will investigate three component elements: the law of belligerent occupation, historical case studies of occupation, and Joint and Army doctrine. The first part of this analysis is a review of the law of belligerent occupation. The review of the law serves three purposes. First, it defines the legal circumstances that constitute a belligerent occupation. Second, it establishes the essential tasks that the law requires of the occupying power. Third, it sets the minimum standard to evaluate the success or failure of all occupations.

1

The second part of this study is a case study of previous occupations. The monograph examines three historical cases of U.S. military occupation: the occupation of Germany after World War II, the occupation of Panama in 1990, and the occupation of Iraq in 2003. The primary focus of this part of the study is an examination of the occupation of Germany after World War II. First, the study investigates the detailed planning that led to the occupation of Germany. Second, it considers the successes and failures in that planning, which provides key lessons learned for planners of today. Third, it tracks the evolution of the doctrine of occupation that followed World War II. The study then compares the occupation of Germany with the more recent occupations of Panama and Iraq to help determine the essential tasks of such missions.

The third point of inquiry examines the doctrine of occupation. This review is designed to determine whether current doctrine adequately addresses the requirements of occupation that the first two parts of the study have generated. This portion of the monograph identifies the shortfalls in current doctrine as compared to the requirements of the law and the lessons of history. The review includes *Field Manuals (FM) 3-0, Operations; 3-07, Stability and Support Operations*; and *41-10, Civil Affairs Operations*; as well as *Joint Publications (JP) 3-0, Doctrine for Joint Operations; 3-07 Joint Doctrine for Military Operations Other than War, and 3-57 Joint Doctrine for Civil-Military Operations. JP 3-0*[1] classifies post-conflict operations as operations other than war (OOTW).[2] As occupation is a post-conflict operation, military OOTW doctrine should logically encompass its requirements. This examination of current doctrine will reveal whether it adequately addresses the occupation mission. The

---

[1] Chairman, Joint Chiefs of Staff, *Joint Publication 3-0 Doctrine for Joint Operations*, Washington, D.C. 9 Sept 1993, III-31. The classification of post-conflict operations as OOTW is found in the 1993 edition. In the 2001 version of JP 3-0 this classification is omitted.

2 Although Joint Doctrine uses the term military operations other than war (MOOTW), the Army uses the term Stability and Support Operations (SASO). According to *JP 1-02*, MOOTW is operations that encompass the use of military capabilities across the range of military operations short of war. These military actions can be applied to complement any combination of the other instruments of national power and occur before, during, and after war. *FM 3-07* defines SASO as the use of military capabilities for any purpose other than war. The definitions are basically the same, for purposes in this monograph, Stability and Support Operations will be the term that is used. Colonel Fastabend offers a good account of the evolution of terminology; see David Fastabend, "The Categorization of Conflict", *Parameters*, 75-87 (1997).

study will also analyze the evolution of the doctrine of military occupation since World War II and determine what lessons from prior doctrine may be applicable today.

Finally, the monograph identifies shortfalls in current doctrine and recommending critical changes. These changes, if adopted will ensure that the U.S. military is better prepared to execute the occupation mission following future conflicts, and will serve the very real needs facing the nation today.

CHAPTER 2

THE LAW OF BELLIGERENT OCCUPATION

Introduction

International law both defines belligerent occupation and places requirements and constraints on the occupying power. Understanding the international law of belligerent occupation is therefore critical to determining the specified military tasks that occupation requires military to perform. The analysis of the law of belligerent occupation focuses on three critical areas. The first section of the analysis looks at the origins of the law. The second section discusses the legal definition of belligerent occupation. The final section determines the specified tasks the occupying power must legally perform. This analysis demonstrates five pillars of occupation that provides a foundation to evaluate how the military has executed prior occupations as well as to develop a model of legally required specified tasks for future occupations.

History of Current Law

Two primary documents lay the foundation for the law of belligerent occupation. The first is the 18 October 1907 Hague Convention IV Respecting the Laws and Customs of War on Land (HR).[3] The second is the 12 August 1949 Geneva Convention Relative to the Protection of Civilian Persons in Time

---

[3] Hague Convention Number IV Respecting the Laws and Customs of War on Land, 18 October 1907. Further reference to this Hague Convention will be as HR.

of War (GC).[4] The Hague Convention sums up the century of legal and military debate that preceded its passage. As such, it serves as the foundation for subsequent international law pertaining to the protection of persons during armed conflict. It also provides specific rules regarding property, finance, and general government administration, and offers guidance for military occupation. The Geneva Convention supplements The Hague rules and provides more detailed requirements for the treatment of civilians.

The occupation rules found in the Hague Convention evolved from a century of evolving custom and debate. Although the distinction between annexation and occupation occurred in the middle of the 18th century, the legal separation of the two terms did not develop until after the Napoleonic wars.[5] As early as 1809, Russia required Swedish citizens to take an oath of allegiance.[6] This was a clear step towards the recognition of the concept of occupation. Although current international law prevents the occupying power from forcing civilians to take a coercive oath of allegiance, the Russian efforts were a marked attempt to control the people of an occupied land.[7]

In 1828, United States Supreme Court Chief Justice John Marshall also countered traditional notions of the outcome of international armed conflict when he found that the fate of a conquered nation did not lay with annexation but instead with temporary military occupation followed by a peace agreement.[8] In *American Insurance Company v. Canter*, he wrote, "[t]he usage of the world is, if a nation

---

[4] Geneva Convention Relative to the Protection of Civilian Persons in Time of War, 12 August 1949. Further references will be referred to as GC.

[5] Gerhard Von Glahn, *The Occupation of Enemy Territory* (Minneapolis: The University of Minnesota press, 1957), 7.

[6] Ibid, 7.

[7] Annexation is generally covered in Von Glahn's background on the international law of military occupation. In the first half of the 18th century conquest of enemy territory equated to an annexation of the conqueror's territory. The land now being under the conqueror's control, he was able to do as he pleased in the occupied area. A greater analysis of annexation and occupation can be found in Graber, Doris A., *The Development of the Law of Belligerent Occupation 1863-1914*, (New York: Columbia University Press, 1949), 340-343.

[8] Annexation of territory is a *permanent* appropriation of territory; whereas an occupation is the *temporary* control over another sovereign state (emphasis is mine). In fact the current U.S. interpretation of international law says, "Being an incident of war, military occupation confers upon the invading force the means of exercising control for the period of occupation. It does not transfer the sovereignty to the occupant, but simply the authority or power to exercise some of the rights of sovereignty....It is therefore unlawful for a belligerent occupant to annex occupied territory or to create a new State therein while hostilities are still in progress." Department of the Army, *Field Manual 27-10, The Law of Land Warfare* (Washington, D.C.: Department of the

be not entirely subdued, to consider the holding of conquered territory as mere military occupation, until

its fate shall be determined at the treaty of peace." [9] Chief Justice Marshall's statement directly

contradicted popular custom at the time, which had held that the conquered land immediately became the

property of the conquering state.

In 1844, Germany became the first country to publish a document noting the importance of

occupation. [10] The 1863 the United States followed suit, laying the foundations for the concept of military

occupation in U.S. Army Manual, *Instructions for the Government of Armies of the United States in the

Field*, commonly known as the Lieber Code. [11] The Lieber Code also led the way for numerous military

manuals addressing the topic of warfare and occupation, including the European Brussels Declaration of

1874 and the Oxford Manual of 1880, laying the foundations for international consensus on the rules of

land warfare. The 1899 and 1907 Hague Conventions Respecting the Laws and Customs of War on Land

ultimately derived many of their provisions directly from the Brussels Declaration. All of these

foundational documents legally recognized the act of occupation, and the rules they established for the

occupying power remained unchanged until after World War II.

Although the 1907 Hague Convention certainly had its critics and challengers in its time, its

provisions lasted throughout both World War I and World War II and continue to this day. [12] The events

of World War II led the impetus for changes in the law of armed conflict to better protect civilians from

the hazards of war. The Geneva Conventions of 1949 attempted to clarify some of the more vague issues

---

Army, 1956), 140. The issue between annexation and occupation is far from over. Benvenisti argues that the Israeli occupations in the West Bank, Gaza, Golan and East Jerusalem amount to an annexation. See, Benvenisti, Eyal, *The International Law of Occupation*, (Princeton, Princeton University Press, 1993), 112, 123-129.

[9] American Insurance Company v. Canter, 26 U.S. 511 (Pet.) (1828).

[10] Von Glahn. 8.

[11] Ibid.

[12] Von Glahn, 7-23. The German document is Hefter, August Wilhem, *Das europäische Völkerrecht der Gegenwart*, 1844. An interesting thesis that argues a slightly less significance to the Leiber Code, Grant R. Doty, "The United States and the Development of the Laws of Land Warfare," *Military Law Review 156* (June1998): 224-255.

from the 1907 Hague Conventions as well as address specific issues raise by the conduct of nations during World War II. Taken together, they constitute current law for the conduct of military occupations, a concept that international law has specifically recognized for nearly a century. This international law provides the foundation to further examine the exact meaning of the term, belligerent occupation.

Definition of Belligerent Occupation

The 1907 Hague Convention specifically defines belligerent occupation. "Territory is considered occupied when it is actually placed under the authority of the hostile army. The occupation extends only to the territory where such authority has been established and can be exercised."[13] This simple definition does not provide much internal detail. To determine when occupation occurs instead requires analysis of the circumstances which trigger the definition.

Although the definition does not specify when a force becomes an occupying power, the common interpretation presupposes both invasion and firm control of the country at issue.[14] An invasion alone is not an occupation. For example, air forces can attack a country from the air, naval forces can attack from the sea, and land forces can rapidly advance through a country, all without providing firm control of the territory being attacked. Only with firm control does an invasion create an occupation, as control allows the exercise of authority. In addition, the invasion does not necessarily need to be resisted. If the invader assumes control without resistance, then occupation still exists.[15] The Hague Convention does not specify that resistance is required.[16]

---

[13] HR, Art. 42.

[14] Department of the Army, *Field Manual 27-10, The Law of Land Warfare* (Washington, D.C.: Department of the Army, 1956), 138.

[15] Ibid. Von Glahn argues against the assumption of invasion, and argues that in addition to occupation based on a hostile invasion in time of war there are also two additional types of occupation. The first is occupation following the complete surrender of an enemy force that no longer has armed forces. The second is the occupation of a neutral that takes place as a plea of military necessity, usually following the liberation of any enemy. Von Glahn, 27.

[16] HR, Art. 42. Additionally *FM 27-10*, paragraph 355, states "Military occupation is a question of fact." Paragraph 357 states, "In a strict legal sense no proclamation of military occupation is necessary…The practice of the United States is to make this fact known by proclamation." Once the elements are met for an occupation it is a question of fact, not law, thus a proclamation is not required.

The concept of firm control of a territory also requires explanation to be useful. The size of the force used itself is immaterial, and should be based on an analysis of the situation. *Field Manual 27-10* succinctly clarifies these issues, "The number of troops necessary to maintain effective occupation will depend on various considerations such as the disposition of the inhabitants, the number and density of the population, the nature of the terrain, and similar factors."[17]

Essential Tasks

An established working definition of what constitutes an occupation permits one to examine what tasks must be accomplished during the occupation mission. As the legal documents that set out the requirements are both lengthy and difficult to understand, it is more useful to synthesize the legal requirements into a model that delineates both mission essential tasks and collective tasks that the occupying force must be prepared to perform.

The five mission essential tasks set forth in the Hague and Geneva Conventions are as follows: (1) Restore and ensure public order and safety,[18] (2) provide medical care, supplies and subsistence,[19] (3) ensure the care and education of children,[20] (4) respect private property and properly manage public property,[21] and (5) provide for the security of the occupying force to facilitate mission accomplishment.[22] These five tasks must be examined to determine the scope of each requirement as well as the implied tasks each contain.

---

[17] Field Manual 27-10, 139.

[18] HR, Art. 42.

[19] GC, Art. 55, 56.

[20] GC, Art. 50.

[21] HR, Art. 23, 52.

[22] GC, Art. 27, 54.

Essential Task: Restore Public Order and Safety

The first essential task is to restore public order and safety. Article 43 of The Hague Conventions states, "The authority of the legitimate power having in fact passed into the hands of the occupant, the latter shall take all measures in his power to restore, and ensure, as far as possible, *public order and safety* (emphasis mine), while respecting, unless absolutely prevented, the laws in force in the country."[23] This task is significant for three reasons. First, it allows the peaceful inhabitants of an occupied territory to continue with their day-to-day lives.[24] Second, it allows the occupant and the local inhabitants to form an agreement to maximize their benefits to both. Third, this task is so broad that it encompasses many of the functions associated with government administration. From this specified task there are four implied tasks that must be addressed in any occupation. Theses implied tasks are 1) reestablishing a domestic security force, 2) providing for the collective protection, 3) administration and enforcement of local laws, and 4) management of the courts, jails, and prisons. The analysis will address these tasks in further detail.

Implied Task: Domestic Security

The first implied task necessary to restoring public order and safety is to reestablish and supervise a form of domestic security. A trusted police force allows for a heightened sense of security in the local populace, reduces crimes against and by the inhabitants, and aids in administering military law. The process of establishing a domestic police force can take some time. Local law enforcement personnel may need to be investigated to ensure that they are reliable, that they are not associated with human rights abuses, and that they are not involved in criminal activity.[25] While international law does not specifically address the need for domestic police forces, their establishment is logically required as part of restoring

---

[23] HR, Art. 43.

[24] Von Glahn, 57.

[25] Daria Wollschlaeger, Post Conflict Governance, Microsoft PowerPoint Presentation, Slide 19, no date present on presentation. LTC Wollschlaeger is the Chair, International & Operational Law Department, The United States Army's Judge Advocate General's School. Presentation is on file with author.

8

public order and safety.[26] Other tasks must be conducted in order to ensure for the collective protection of the population and the occupant.

Implied Task: Collective Protection

The second implied task, providing for the collective protection of the inhabitants of the occupied country, is directly related to the establishment of a domestic police force but greater in scope. The collective protection of inhabitants also requires the occupying power to collect weapons and ammunition that may pose harm to the inhabitants and conflict with the occupant's goals. Other sub-tasks of collective protection include restricting the movement of the population,[27] controlling the sale of liquor and narcotics, controlling and restricting methods of communications,[28] controlling modes of transportation, and restoring and controlling public utilities.[29] This could be further interpreted as the reestablishment and manning of local fire departments and emergency services as well as public utilities as additional implied tasks. Although some of these tasks appear onerous and detailed, particularly for the occupying power, performing them serves the additional purpose of ensuring the best possible relations between the occupying power and the inhabitants of the occupied country. Providing the security for the inhabitant and the occupant is the first pillar of public order and safety. The next pillar addresses the collective protection of the inhabitants and how it cannot occur without the use of local laws.

Implied Task: Administration and Enforcement of Local Laws

The third implied task is to review the local laws in order to enforce, suspend or repeal them and enact new laws in their place as needed. The Geneva Convention provides, "[t]he penal laws of the occupied territory shall remain in force, with the exception that they may be suspended by the Occupying

---

[26] Von Glahn, 57.

[27] Ibid, 141.

[28] Ibid, 139.

[29] Wollschlaeger, Slide 33.

Power in case where they constitute a threat to its security."[30] Although it is United States policy to use local laws unless military necessity requires otherwise,[31] there can be valid reasons for suspension of local laws. For example, an occupying power may suspend or repeal laws that are discriminatory or counter to the occupant's beliefs and goals within the occupied territory.[32] Although not commonly done, the occupying power may also enact their own laws in the occupied country, as both Germany and Allied forces did during World War II.[33] Clearly, certain procedures must be adhered to ensure any new laws are both effective and obeyed. Such procedures would include giving notice to the populace in their native language(s), publishing the laws in writing, and ensuring that new laws are not applied in an *ex post facto* fashion.[34] The last pillar addressed is a system to deal with criminals.

Implied Task: Courts, Jails, Prisons

The fourth implied task to the restoration of public order and safety is supervision of courts, jails, and prisons.[35] The Geneva Convention provides, "[t]he necessity of ensuring effective administration of justice, the tribunals of the occupied territory shall continue to function in respect to all offenses covered by the said laws."[36] The occupying power has considerable latitude to use a variety of courts, tribunals, and local government systems to adequately enforce and administer the law. First, the occupying power may use the indigenous courts in order to enforce the domestic law of the occupied state, although the laws enforced there are only against the inhabitants and not the occupying power. The Geneva Conventions also provide the occupying power the ability to establish new courts to administer justice

---

[30] GC, Art. 64.

[31] Field Manual 27-10, 142.

[32] Ibid, 143.

[33] Von Glahn, 99-100.

[34] Morris Greenspan, *The Modern Law of Land Warfare*, (Berkeley, CA; University of California Press. 1959), 221.

[35] GC Art. 64- 78 covers courts and penal systems.

[36] GC, Art. 64.

over the inhabitants when the justice system in the occupied state is dysfunctional.[37] In addition, the

occupying power may establish courts within the occupied state to deal with offenses against the

occupant, or to deal with violations of the occupant's laws in the occupied nation.[38] Finally, the

conventions specifically permit the occupying power to remove officials from public office who refuse to

fulfill their duties.[39]

In addition to establishing an effective judicial system, the occupying power must take charge of

the jails and prisons to ensure the safety of both the inhabitants and the occupying forces.[40] While

obviously those who were jailed prior to occupation could also pose a threat during occupation, the

occupying power must review those imprisoned at the time of the occupation to ensure that those jailed

did not include persons who were wrongly accused or political prisoners from the former regime.[41]

Essential Task: Provide Subsistence, Medical Care and Supplies

The second essential task from international law is to provide the population subsistence, medical

care and supplies.[42] The nature of war invariably stresses the occupied country's systems for providing

for the basic needs of its people. By properly planning for these unavoidable tasks before the conflict

begins, the occupant can prevent undue hardship and drain on their own resources while still ensuring the

welfare of the civilian population. Four implied tasks stem from the requirement to provide medical care

---

[37] Ibid.

[38] GC, Art. 64-78

[39] GC, Art. 54.

[40] This is interpreted from security measures for the populace and the occupant. GC Art.78 states, "If the Occupying power considers it necessary, for *imperative reasons of security, to take safety measures concerning protection of persons*, it may, at the most, subject them to assigned residence or to internment." Emphasis is mine. *FM 27-10* paragraph 432 mandates security of the forces and the duty of the inhabitants to carry on in peaceful manner.

[41] John F. Burns, "Threats and Responses: The Great Escapes; Hussein and Mobs Virtually Empty Iraq's Prisons," New York Times, 21 October 2002, Sec. A, 1. Although in the Iraq, many people who disagreed with the Saddam Hussein Regime were imprisoned, there also appears to be many that were true criminals. Procedures must be in place to ensure those imprisoned are just. As Burns' article points out many criminals were released for dubious reason, which begs the questions of legitimate imprisonment in the first place.

[42] GC, Art. 56.

and subsistence. These tasks are: 1) the distribution of food, medical supplies, and clothing; 2) the production and processing of food; 3) support of relief organizations; 4) and the (re)establishment of medical facilities and medical supply stocks.

Implied Task: Distribution of Food, Medical Supplies, Clothing

The first implied task is to obtain and distribute requisite food, medical supplies, clothing, and other humanitarian aid for civilian relief.[43] The scope of this requirement will necessarily vary with the number of people requiring support and the severity of the people's need. The length of the war in the area and the amount of infrastructure destruction will affect the amounts of supplies that the occupying power must provide. The occupying power may even be forced to ration supplies based on its ability to provide subsistence and care to all who require it. Providing food in the short is one challenge, another challenge is ensuring for the subsistence in the long term.

Implied Task: Production and Processing of Food

The second implied task is to encourage indigenous industries involved in the production and processing of food to continue operations.[44] This task is critical for several reasons. First, it allows for the occupied country to better transition to self-sustaining in the future. Second, it reduces the dependency that the occupied country has on the occupying power for basic food needs. Finally, doing so eliminates the significant burden on the occupying power that providing and distributing food can place. The occupant does not have to be alone in these efforts. Assistance can come from other agencies interested in the welfare of the population.

---

[43] GC, Art. 55

[44] GC, Art. 55. Art. 55, it states " To the fullest extent of *the means available to it*, the occupying power has the duty of ensuring the food and medical supplies of the population; it should, in particular, bring in the necessary foodstuffs, medical stores and other articles if *the resources of the occupied territory are inadequate.* Emphasis is mine. Also see Von Glahn, 145.

Implied Task: Support of Relief Organizations

The third implied task, encouraging the support of relief organizations, likewise relieves some of the burden of caring for the civilian population from the occupying power.[45] Relief organizations such as the International Committee of the Red Cross (ICRC) can assist in providing some of the medical and basic subsistence needs of the civilian population. It is important that the occupying power realize, however, that the services relief organizations provide do not relieve the occupant of the responsibility of ensuring that those services are provided.

Implied Task: Medical Facilities and Medical Supply Stocks

The final implied task to providing food, subsistence, and medical care and supplies is to reestablish existing medical facilities and to ensure existing medical supply stocks are properly apportioned and distributed.[46] Doing so avoids undue strain on deployed military medical services and facilitates transition of medical services to effective domestic control. Additionally, ensuring that medical services and supplies are being properly distributed to the populace has the additional benefit of reducing the likelihood that needed supplies will end up in the hands of resistance or insurgent forces still operating in the occupied territory.

Essential Task: Care and Education of Children

The third essential task of an occupying power is to ensure for the care and education of children. The Geneva Convention mandates that "[t]he Occupying Power shall, with the cooperation of the national and local authorities, facilitate the proper working of all institutions devoted to the care and education of children."[47] The same provision specifically directs identification of children, reunion with parents, care

---

[45] GC, Art 59, 60.

[46] Von Glahn, 142.

[47] GC, Art. 50. GC. Under GC, Art. 6, the duties for certain provisions cease after 1 year, one of those is GC, Art. 50. The Additional Protocol to the Geneva Convention (Protocol Additional to the Geneva Conventions of 12 August 1949, and relating to the Protection of Victims of International Armed Conflicts (Protocol I), 8 June 1977) nullify this one year provision, but the United States has not ratified the Additional Protocol of 1977. Thought the requirement goes away after a year of occupation, international pressure and media coverage may deem that the care and education of children would continue past the one year requirement.

of orphans, as well as preferential medical treatment and subsistence for children under the age of 15, expectant mothers, and mothers with children under the age of seven.[48]

There are two implied tasks that can be derived from these requirements. First, the occupying power must ensure that education facilities are provided and properly functioning. As with providing food and medical care, this task will vary with the type of country occupied, the status of the country before the conflict, the length of the conflict prior to occupation, and the wartime damage to civilian infrastructure. Facilities that were in use before the occupation must be examined to determine if they can still be used to meet the needs of children's education and be relocated and rebuilt as necessary. Providing teachers will also be necessary, and the occupying power is responsible for finding acceptable teachers, preferably those who share the same language and culture as the children.[49]

Essential Task: Manage and Respect Property

The final essential task of the occupying power, to respect private property and manage public property, contains far fewer specific legal requirements. For private property, the Hague Convention requires the occupying power to protect it and forbids its confiscation.[50] The requirements for public property are less specific. The Hague Convention states:

> The occupying State shall be regarded only as administrator and usufructurary of public buildings, real estate, forests and agricultural estates belonging to the hostile State, and situated in the occupied country. It must safeguard the capital of these properties, and administer them in accordance with the rules of usufruct. The property of municipalities, that of institutions dedicated to religion, charity and education, the arts and sciences, even when State property, shall be treated as private property. All seizure of, destruction or willful damage done to institutions of this character, historic monuments, works of art and science, is forbidden, and should be made the subject of legal proceedings.[51]

---

[48] Ibid.

[49] Ibid.

[50] HR, Art. 46.

[51] HR, Art. 55, 56.

There are three implied tasks that can be derived from this provision. First, the occupying power must distinguish between types of property, and must determine whether property is privately or publicly owned.[52] Secondly, based upon this determination, the occupying power must determine if there is military value associated with the property. Property such as rail yards, forts, and airfields have direct military value that the occupying power may capitalize on as necessary, as control over such property facilitates the mission of the occupying power and prevents its use by any opposing or insurgent force.[53] Property that has no military value must still be safeguarded and properly administered to prevent its damage or waste.[54] Thirdly, the occupying power must take affirmative steps to prevent damage or waste to that property that has no direct military value.[55] Doing so has the collateral effect of promoting good will among the occupied people and prevents valuables from falling into the hands of the opposing force.

Essential Task: Provide Security for the Occupying Force

Although the task to provide security for the occupying forces is not directly stated in the Hague and Geneva Conventions, it can be inferred from the law. HR Art 42 states, "Territory is considered occupied when it is actually placed under the authority of the hostile army. The occupation extends only to the territory where such authority has been established and can be exercised."[56] Two points from this article demonstrate the essential nature of providing security for the occupying forces. First, the article states the importance of territory being placed under the authority of a hostile army. Secondly, the article further qualifies the nature of the authority mandating the establishment and exercising of the authority. It can therefore be inferred that if authority cannot be achieved, then occupation has not been achieved. Security for the occupying force is therefore a prerequisite to legal occupation, for without the proper

---

[52] GC, Art. 53.

[53] Von Glahn, 176-180.

[54] HR, Art. 55.

[55] Von Glahn, 180-183.

[56] HR, Art. 42.

security, it is possible for the authority of the occupation to falter and prevent the occupying force's ability to execute essential tasks. Certainly this requires application as each situation calls for different security requirements.

Summary

The foregoing analysis demonstrates the five pillars of occupation (see Figure 1). The degree of application of each of these tasks may vary on the situation of the given occupation but every occupation addresses these five pillars. This analysis also provides a model in which to evaluate the United States Army's doctrine on occupation. If these tasks are mandatory, then doctrine should address these essential tasks.

The law dictates only a minimum standard. As with any operation, there is the application of forces and action based on the situational analysis. There may be further tasks based on the occupying force and its assessment of the mission. Additionally, although international law prescribes tasks to be completed, it does not tell how to complete these tasks. This is where an analysis of actual occupations can aid in a complete understanding of the occupations. The next chapter will cover this in further detail.

Restore Public Order and Safety			
Courts, Jails, and Prisons	Local Laws	Collective Protection	Domestic Security
Provide Subsistence, Medical Care and Supplies			
Medical Facilities and Medical Supply Stocks	Support of Relief Organizations	Production and Processing of Food	Distribution of Food, Medical Supplies, Clothing
Care and Education of Children			
Manage and Respect Property			
Provide Security for the Occupying Force			

Figure 1, The Five Pillars of Occupation. Essential tasks mandated by law.

CHAPTER 3

HISTORY

Introduction

Historical case studies demonstrate other additional tasks and a practical understanding of the necessary issues involved. History enables us to see how past planners approached the mission of occupation. The military professionals of other eras handled many complex missions just like the Army is facing today in Afghanistan and Iraq. Lessons from these experiences are a great value for the Army today. The challenge of today is how and what to integrate from these lessons into current and future occupation missions and possibly laying the foundation for the development of doctrine.

This chapter examines three occupations: the U.S. Army in Germany after WWII, the occupation of Panama after the US intervention in 1989, and the occupation of Iraq after the US invasion in March 2003. They were chosen for specific reasons. They all represent occupations in which the United States participated or led a coalition. Germany represents an occupation of great scope and magnitude. Specifically, Germany was an utterly devastated country and its reconstruction was vital to the reconstruction of Europe. Panama was a much smaller scale occupation: the removal of the Manuel Noregia's government in Panama took only days. Finally, the current occupation in Iraq contrasts and highlights lessons from the other two case studies. Operation Iraqi Freedom and the subsequent occupation are unique due to the United States' unprecedented position in the world and its willingness to enforce this action without the consensus of world leaders. Additionally, Iraq, like Germany, was suppressed for years of totalitarian rule and additionally depressed economically by years of United Nations imposed sanctions.

World War II

Although some will argue that the tasks associated with an occupation are better depicted by the recent stability operations that the United States has executed in the 1990s,[57] the occupation of Germany after World War II demonstrates many lessons due to the length of the operation, the scope of tasks conducted, planning, and transition back to a German government. This analysis offers eight points of analysis which could further add to the framework for occupation: 1) the structure of military government operations; 2) the level of preparation before the actual occupation; 3) the transition from combat forces towards a constabulary force; 4) the denazification of Germany; 5) the promulgation of democratization; 6) the efforts to care and feed for the German people; a perspective on how to handle millions of displaced persons; 8) the ongoing dispute between the Department of State and the Defense establishment on who should be in charge and offers one method to solve.

The Structure of Military Government

The first lesson that the occupation of Germany offers is a organizational structure for military government forces. Specifically, two aspects of the organizational structure could serve as a model for future operations. The first was the staff and planning organization of military government within the European Theater. The second was the military government organization in the field.

The overarching military government organization was headed out of Washington by the Civil Affairs Division (CAD).[58] A corresponding theater organization was called the European Civil Affairs Division (ECAD).[59] Although the Supreme Allied Commander of the European Theater of Operations was overall in charge of the military government operation, he delegated the tasks to his Deputy Military

---

[57] Conrad C. Crane and W. Andrew Terrill, "Reconstruction Iraq: Insights, Challenges, and Mission for Military Forces in a Post-Conflict Scenario" (Monograph, Strategic Studies Institute, U.S. Army War College, Carlisle, PA), 2003.

[58] Earl F. Ziemke, *The U.S. Army in the Occupation of Germany 1944-1946* (Washington, D.C.: Center of Military History United States Army, 1975), 14-17.

[59] Ibid, 68.

Governor.[60] The deputy's staff formed the ECAD. This model of the CAD and ECAD national and

theater level organizations that could be useful models for other occupations.

The command structure offers additional lessons to today's military. Initially, the heart of

planning for military government of Germany within ECAD was the German Country Unit. Later the

U.S. groups Control Council absorbed the German Country Unit as the Control Council was established

after the allied occupational split of Germany. Due to a poor transition and overconfidence, U.S. Group

Control Council experienced difficulties that the German Country Unit did not. The U.S. Group Control

Council struggled for control with the G-5 of the U.S. Forces, European Theater (USFET) for direction of

the Military Government programs.[61] Eventually this was resolved when the Office of Military

Government United States (OMGUS) was stood up to alleviate their differences.[62] Although successful

like the CAD and ECAD at higher levels, the U.S. Groups Control Council demonstrated the importance

of unity of effort and continuity by the Military Government staffs.[63]

The military government organization in the field offers a good method for employment of forces.

In the field the military government units organized into five types of detachments. The E detachment

was the largest in size but the fewest in number, consisting of more than 100 officers and numerous

enlisted soldiers, with a spectrum of expertise.[64] The E Detachment was able to take over *Länder* (states),

Provinzen (provinces), and *Stadtkreise* (large cities). The F Detachments were slightly smaller than the E

---

[60] Ibid, 224.

[61] Additional G-5 elements were located in the Army Groups, Army level, and Corps.

[62] Zink, 46.

[63] Once SHAEF dissolved USFET was created. The military government chains of command followed two different lines under USFET. The first chain ran from Eisenhower (Commander, USFET) through the Third and Seventh Army Commanders. The second was a technical chain of command that ran through LTG Lucius Clay (Deputy Commander USFET and Deputy Military Governor) to the theater G-5, military district headquarter G-5, and to ultimately the military government detachments. See Walter M. Hudson, "The U.S. Military Government and Democratic Reform and Denazification in Bavaria, 1945-47," Master's Thesis, U.S. Army Command and General Staff College, Ft. Leavenworth, KS, 2001, 15.

[64] E Detachments specialties ranged from mining, forestry, oil refining, fisheries, public safety, public health, government and administration, food, agriculture, public finance, banking, insurance, public works, public utilities, courts and legal systems, education, religious affairs, intelligence, transportation, communications, monuments, fine arts and archives, and trade and industry. See Zink, 57-65

Detachment and had a greater ratio of enlisted to officers. The F Detachments could take over *Regierungsbezirke* (districts) and large *Stadtkreise*. The C Detachments covered smaller *Regierungsbezirke* and larger *Landkreise* (rural counties). The H and I Detachments were the most numerous, though only consisted of four to six officers. They were designed for the smallest *Landkreise* and the smallest *Stadtkreise*. H and I Detachment specialties were largely area dependent and they adjusted to fit the problems in specific areas.[65]

Much of today's Civil Affairs team structure originated in these teams created for Germany.[66] However, the distinction between Germany and today is that today's Civil Affairs branch has a much wider complement of missions that they can perform.[67] Additionally, the team and command and control structures offer a possible method for a future occupation. Lastly, the successes of the organizational structure only came with maximum preparation and planning for the upcoming occupation.

Preparation

One of the most applicable lessons to draw from the occupation of Germany is the importance of comprehensive and early planning. In 1920, Colonel Irwin L. Hunt, Officer in Charge of Civil Affairs for Third Army after World War I stated "The American army of occupation lacked both training and organization to guide the destinies of the nearly one million civilians whom the fortunes of war had placed under its temporary sovereignty."[68] Colonel Hunt's published report that influenced the occupation planners during World War II, who did not want to repeat the mistakes of the previous occupation of Germany.[69] In the mid 1930s the U.S. Army War College took the initial lessons from the

---

[65] Zink, 60.

[66] Department of the Army, *Field Manual 41-10 Civil Affairs Operations*, (Washington, D.C.: Department of the Army, 14 February 2000). Chapter 3 details the organization, capabilities, and functions of Civil Affairs units.

[67] The mission for military government was occupation or civil administration. The current mission areas for civil affairs are Foreign National Support, Populace and Resource Control, Humanitarian Assistance, Military Civic Action, Emergency Services, Support to Civil Administration. See *FM 41-10* Chapter 2.

[68] Ziemke, 3.

[69] Ibid, 3.

Hunt Report and began looking at military government and administration of occupied territory. A new intensity was added to the War College's efforts as the Axis Powers early successes in WWII caused governments to disappear, go into exile, or become collaborators, thus pushing the issue of military occupations to the forefront.

The U.S. Army took two fundamental steps to prepare for successful military occupations. The first was the creation of two field manuals, FM 27-10, the Law of Land Warfare, and FM 27-5, Military Government, which are discussed in more detail in Chapter Four.

The U.S. Army's second step created a school designed to train personnel in military government. The school is important for three reasons. First, the creation of the school made the Army responsible for military government. President Roosevelt designated the early role belonged to the Army.[70] Second, it gave a method for selection and training of the specialists needed to perform the military governance mission. The initial program established solely at the University of Virginia fell extremely short in producing the numbers of trained soldiers who would ultimately be needed to conduct the military governance mission.[71] In late 1942, the Military Government Division expanded the number of trainees by creating the Civil Affairs Training Program (CATP).[72] This program allowed students to train at certified universities.[73] Third, the school established dialogue and a forum in which to plan the military occupation missions.

With the establishment of the school was the formation of the concurrent U.S. Army's Civil Affairs Division. This Division reported directly to the Secretary of War on "all matters except those of a

---

[70] Ziemke, 22. In a letter dated 10 November 1943 from President Roosevelt to Secretary of War Henry Stimson, President Roosevelt stated, "Although other agencies are preparing themselves for the work that must be done in connection with relief and rehabilitation of liberated areas, it is quite apparent that if prompt results are to be obtained the Army will have to assume the initial burden."

[71] Ibid, 8.

[72] Ibid, 18

[73] Ibid, 18-20.

military nature and to represent the Secretary of War to outside agencies."[74] Shortly after this, Secretary Stimson mandated that the Civil Affairs Division ensured that all occupation plans contain planning for civil affairs. Stimson's mandate gave the civil affairs sections within the planning staffs a boost in credibility and purpose.[75]

The early planning, establishment of a school and training program, and the establishment of a national level Civil Affairs agency are useful ideas from the past that have been or could help future occupations. Clearly, the successful preparations during the early stages of WWII reveal the importance of early recognition and planning for a potential occupation. Additionally, the current U.S. Army has learned from the successful occupation of Germany (and others occupations) and created a standing Civil Affairs force that is responsible for the Civil Administration mission.[76] Furthermore, the current civil affairs community has established schools and training programs to educate and train civil affairs soldiers on all their possible missions. Both aspects have a direct connection to the efforts prior to WWII. Possibly, another lesson from the preparation prior to the occupation of Germany that should be integrated into the current force is a national or Army level agency or staff position that has oversight or directly responsible for the Civil Affairs mission.[77]

Constabulary Force

The U.S. Constabulary Force was established to "reduce the requirements for U.S. manpower and expense."[78] Before the end of the war, the Army did not know the level of resistance and difficulty that the Germans would assemble. Initially, security vacuums and rogue bands of German military units were

---

[74] Ibid, 17.

[75] Ibid, 25.

[76] *FM 41-10*, Chapter 2.

[77] Similar to the Civil Affairs Division. Civil Affairs currently falls under the Special Operation Community with over sight by the U.S. Special Operations Command. No permanent staff is located in the Department of Defense or Army Staff. See *FM 41-10*, Chapter 4.

[78] Zeimke, 325.

great concerns. These concerns turned out to be overstated. Additionally, pressure from the home front

urged officials to speed the American withdrawal and bring the troops back home.[79]

American troops numbered over 1.6 million in Germany on V-E Day. This force quickly

initiated occupation duties, making its presence known throughout the American sector.[80] As Earl

Ziemke states the "combat forces became military government security troops,"[81] manning checkpoints,

monitoring border crossings, and enforcing curfew restrictions. In response to the pressure withdrawal

American forces, General Marshall strongly urged General Eisenhower to consider a police type

occupation force. Marshall suggested the possibility of using foreign troops to conduct the constabulary

force.[82] Eisenhower acted on Marshall's suggestions but the request for foreign forces failed because of

substantial concerns of language problems and increasing expenses.[83] As a result Eisenhower established

the U.S. Constabulary force in October 1945.

The Constabulary force was created from division cavalry groups. Based on a ratio of one solider

per 450 Germans, the force was planned to number 38,000 soldiers, but reached its peak at 31,000.[84] The

Constabulary plan would reduce the required occupation manning structure by 81,000 soldiers. It was

envisioned to receive specialized training in law enforcement, conduct raids, serve as a quick reaction

---

[79] Ibid, 320.

[80] "Directive to the Commander-in-Chief of the United States Forces of Occupation Regarding the Military Government of Germany," also known as JCS 1067, Found in United States Department of State, *Documents on Germany 1944-1985*, (Washington, DC: Office of Historian, US Department of State, 1985), 15-32. JCS 1067 was a policy of "short term and military character, in order not to prejudice whatever ultimate policies may later be determined upon." Its object was to establish a "stern, all-powerful military administration of a conquered country, based on its unconditional surrender, impressing the Germans with their military defeat and the futility of any further aggression." See Ziemke, 104.

[81] Ziemke, 320.

[82] Ibid, 339.

[83] Ibid, 340.

[84] Ibid, 341.

force, and train a new German Police force. Elite, hand picked soldiers marked with distinctive uniforms would fill the positions in the force.[85]

The significance of the creation of the Constabulary force is twofold. First, its creation alleviated personnel requirements to conduct the occupation mission. Second, the Constabulary allowed for a better overall focus on occupation duties. The separation of law enforcement duties and security duties from the other occupation tasks allowed other military government forces to concentrate on denazification, democratization, and establishing the new German government. As seen in Operation Iraqi Freedom the desire to have U.S. troops returned home is a consistent theme and will be a condition that planners will need to deal with in the future. Additionally, the creation of a Constabulary force demonstrates a method of separation of duties and task organizing appropriately to better facilitate the entire occupation mission.

Denazification

In all past U.S. occupations, the legacy of the past governments has remained and created conditions that the United States had to manage. Germany had the imprint of Nazism that had to be erased. Denazification required a purging and punishing those who were Nazis, and enabling Germany to function on its own again. The controlling document for the occupation, JCS 1067 stated, "All members of the Nazi Party who have been more than nominal participants, all active supporters of Nazism or militarism and all other persons hostile to Allied purposes will be removed and excluded from public office and positions of importance in quasi-public and private enterprises."[86] Military Government Law No. 8 went even further prohibiting the "employment of Nazi party members in business in any capacity other than common labor."[87]

---

[85] ibid, 341.

[86] Ziemke, 382. The Morgenthau Plan, created by U.S. Secretary of Treasury Henry Morgenthau, called for the post-war Germany to be stripped of its industry and return to an agriculture based state. Early in the policy development process the JCS 1067 followed the guidelines laid out in the Morgenthau Plan. See, Ziemke, 102 and Zink, xi-18.

[87] Ibid, 382.

The denazification policy had its impacts as military government soldiers implemented it. Local military government detachments disqualified sorely needed doctors, teachers, and policemen. In one instance, the Bremen detachment disqualified 400 of 1600 police officers.[88] In late 1945 an appeals process ultimately reinstated many who had been only nominal members in the party.[89] Those considered more hardened were, at least, theoretically, subject to greater punishment. In accomplishing this distinction, the occupation forces attempted to recognize the distinction between those who were those hardened members of the Nazi Party and those who were members for self-preservation or convenience. Military government forces had to execute other tasks to remove Nazism from Germany. The education system was stripped of any hint of Nazism. Accordingly, OMGUS rewrote textbooks and removed suspect teachers.[90] OMGUS promoted freedom of the press and airways and ensured their control by personnel with anti-Nazi backgrounds.

Democratization

Concomitant with denazification were the efforts by the military government forces to democratic and the rebuild of the German government. JCS 1067 called for Germany to be rebuilt on a democratic structure, which started quickly in the United States sector.[91] Local elections for towns numbering fewer than 20,000 people were held in January 1946. Towns with population between 20,000 and 100,000 held elections March and May 1946. Given the level of destruction throughout Germany and the total collapse of their government, these elections moved with great swiftness. The elections then enabled the local populace to take ownership of their own problems and lessened the resentment that the Germany people had toward the occupying forces.

---

[88] Ibid, 387.

[89] Ibid, 389.

[90] Ziemke, 370.

[91] Zink, 179.

The lessons from the democratization of Germany are three-fold. First, by holding elections, the people focus on acknowledging and correcting their own issues. Second, by initially establishing government at the lowest levels, it is easier to develop a sense of community with common groups and cultures which allows for critical successes early in the occupation. Lastly, the efforts of the military government soldiers in applying democratic reform demonstrate the levels which this may have to be applied in the future. In the case of Germany holding elections and other reconstruction efforts that aided in democratization reveal probable scenarios for future military occupations.

Care and Feeding of the Populace

The basis for any reconstruction effort was the proper care and feeding of the inhabitants. JCS 1067 called for the military government forces to "meet the need of the occupying forces and to ensure the production and maintenance of goods and services required to prevent disease and unrest."[92] Since the German Government had ceased to exist, the duty of providing economic relief also fell upon the military governors. Lieutenant General Lucius Clay, Deputy Military Governor, and his subordinates interpreted the narrow stance that JCS 1067 laid out, feeling that if they could get the German industrial capacity started then the economic benefit from it would aid with the sustenance and relief burden.[93] Consequently, in the U.S. sector LTG Clay ensure that the German factories and mines received a high priority. As a recent study notes, LTG "Clay and his subordinates rapidly and efficiently organized the provision of humanitarian assistance and restarted government services and economic activity. The U.S.

---

[92] JCS 1067, paragraph 5.a., <http://www.usembassy.de/usa/etexts/ga3-450426.pdf> [12 JAN 2004].

[93] JCS 1067 (revision 10 May 1945) still kept the harsh occupation language from the Morgenthau Plan but also allowed the Military Governor to "protect the safety and meet the needs of the occupying forces and assure the production and maintenance of goods and services required to *prevent starvation of such disease and unrest* as would endanger these forces." (Emphasis is mine) Lieutenant General Clay used this loophole to justify large food supplies that were brought into Germany, the reconstruction of the railroads, and the trucks that were given to German businesses on a deferred payment basis. See John Backer, "From Morgenthau Plan to Marshall Plan," Americans as Proconsuls: *United States Military Government in Germany and Japan, 1944-1952*, (Carbondale, IL: Southern Illinois University Press, 1984), 157.

Army's focus on 'getting things moving' was key to minimizing humanitarian suffering and accelerating economic recovery in its zone in the immediate aftermath of World War II."[94]

The care and feeding of the people is a task dictated by the law.[95] The military government leadership in Germany understood the law and its relevant importance. Additionally, they understood that the unrest of the people could quickly cause many additional problems. Lieutenant General Clay, in particular, realized the role of a productive economy in caring for the people. The last lesson to take away from the examples set by care and feeding of the people during the occupation of Germany is the importance of coalition. In the case of Germany, France and the Soviet Union's desires for the reconstruction of Germany did not mirror the United States' goals, which were counter-productive in Germany's ultimate reconstruction.

Displaced persons

Critical in the reconstruction of Germany was the management of displaced persons (DP) in the U.S. sector. The great number of DPs, the requirements the Geneva Convention[96] placed on the Military Government in respect to the DPs, and the attitude of some of the DPs were at issue. The DPs consisted of all types of people, including forced laborers migrated from German controlled areas, Russians who were forced to fight for the Germans, and recovered Allied military personnel. Their entitlements were clothing, shelter, and rations.

The number of DPs in the U.S. zone numbered 2.5 million and the resources needed for this massive number caused great strain on the military government and the German people. The amount of food that all the people received was fixed. The standard DP was required a 2000 calorie per day

---

[94] James Dobbins and et al., *America's Role in Nation Building: From Germany to Iraq* (Santa Monica, CA: Rand: 2003), 22.

[95] GC Art. 50, 55, and 56. Although these laws were not in effect until the United Signed the Convention in 1949, the 1943 *Field Manual 27-5 Military Government and Civil Affairs*, 11, confirms that the United States abided by this parameter even before the law was signed.

[96] GC Art., 79-90. The United States recognized the issue of displaced persons before the signing of the convention in 1949. *Handbook for Military Government in Germany*, 1945, Section III, paragraphs 700-756 state the specifics for dealing with displaced persons in Germany.

allowance. Displaced persons who were recovered allied military personnel received 3600 calories per day, the equivalent of an American soldier.[97] Additionally, the Soviets argued that Soviet DPs should receive the American soldier caloric equivalent.[98] The providers of a substantial amount of the DPs rations came from the German people. Only after the DPs received their required rations would the German people be allowed to receive their share.[99] These entitlements due the DPs strained the German production capability and further hampered the reconstruction efforts in Germany. Military government officials understood the burden caused by the DPs and realized the sooner repatriation of the DPs the quicker the reconstruction of Germany.

The repatriation of the DPs proved difficult as many of the DPs enjoyed living in the DP camps.[100] They were better fed and many had a greater quality of life than they had ever experienced before. So settled did some DPs become that they started to increase their daily demands for food, clothing, and shelter. These increased demands became unsustainable particularly to German populace, since all the DPs necessities were at the expense of the German people. The DPs were also the major contributor to crime, with many of the DPs forming gangs, engaging in looting sprees and in open banditry.[101]

Two lessons come from the military government soldiers dealing with the DPs. First, well-trained low ranking soldiers handled the majority of the DPs and their problems. Ziemke cites one example of a Private First Class running a camp for over 3000 DPs.[102] Relatively low ranking soldiers actively searched for hidden food stores and helped reenergize the stalled German agriculture sector. As

---

[97] Ziemke, 205.

[98] This increase equated to another half million tons of rations. Ziemke, 205.

[99] Ziemke, 203.

[100] Ibid, 240. also see Zink, 108

[101] Zink, 82.

[102] Ibid, 203.

a result of such efforts by September 1945, the original 2.5 million DPs now only numbered 600,000.

The second lesson is military planners must acknowledge the complexity of the DP problem and must

address it in all future occupations. Some DPs may not want to be repatriated, some may demand more

than there allotted shares, and some may be opposed to the established interim government.

Who's in charge?

The last lesson from the occupation of Germany demonstrated that the question over who is in

charge of an occupation is not a new one and offers one possible solution. In the case of Germany,

President Roosevelt settled the debate over who would have authority for military government. Initially,

Department of State and Department of the Interior officials wanted less of a military monopoly on the

control of the schooling and operations. However, President Roosevelt's final ruling came in November,

1943, when he stated, "Although other agencies are preparing themselves for the work that must be done

in connection with relief and rehabilitation of liberated areas, it is quite apparent that if prompt results are

to be obtained the Army will have to assume the initial burden."[103] Continuing, he assigned to the Army

the planning and execution of civil relief and rehabilitation "until civilian agencies are prepared to carry

out the longer range program."[104] Although an issue that occurred in World War II, the debate of who

should be in charge of an occupation was also seen during the Operation IRAQI FREEDOM. The same

debate occurred between the State Department and the Department of Defense. Additionally, President

Roosevelt's ruling 1943 set a precedent that should be still followed today.

Panama

Whereas Germany was a physically devastated country following total world war, Panama,

followed a limited war in 1989-90 was mainly intact. Specifically Operation PROMOTE LIBERTY was

the concurrent civil military operation to Operation JUST CAUSE,[105] the United States mission to restore

---

[103] Ibid, 22.

[104] Ibid, 22.

[105] John T. Fishel, *The Fog of Peace: Planning and Executing the Restoration of Panama,* (Carlisle Barracks, PA: Strategic Studies Institute, U.S. Army War College, 1992), vii.

democracy to the Panama and oust military dictator General Manual Noriega. The occupation of Panama offers six lessons whose prior consideration would benefit future occupations: 1) the recognition of a clear objective for an occupation; 2) the relationship between different agencies within the United States government; 3) the proper role of the current Civil Affairs military professionals; 4) the conduct and integration of the occupation planning process in to the combat plan; 5) the method of unity of command; and 6) the organization and transition for a longer-term civil-military operation.

Objective

The first lesson is the importance of a clear objective. In World War II, the government provided JCS 1067 to provide the objectives for the occupation and reconstruction of Germany. In contrast, the goals for the invasion of Panama were less helpful. As Woodward describes them, "The goals in Panama were obvious: protection of U.S. citizens and interests, and installation of a friendly, democratic government."[106]

Although these objectives were clear and to the point, they also left much room for implementation. Defining the term "democracy" is difficult in an environment that has never known the concept of true democracy. John Fishel argues that a strategy to achieve democracy was never developed.[107] No one planned for a democratic Panama. The military planners planned at the operational level, shying away from the objectives at the strategic level. Equally, the civilian strategists failed to determine a strategy for democracy. Thus, the operational plan never connected back to any strategy.[108] Fishel recommends that this military must be part of this process to develop the strategy, but in a coordinated manner.[109]

---

[106] Bob Woodward, *The Commanders,* (New York: Simon & Schuster, 1991), 85.

[107] Fishel, 5.

[108] Ibid.

[109] Ibid, 66.

This challenge to implement the objectives of military governance is not without its precedent. The same challenges were present as the Army developed doctrine and a School for Military Governance prior to WWII. In the case of the Army if WWII, it stepped forward and recognized the void in planning and attempted to fill it. In Panama, they military avoided it. In both cases the question of the responsibility in military governance arises.

Interagency Process

The question of responsibility leads to the question of the proper interagency coordination between the military and other organizations supporting an occupation. The relationship of the military and the State Department becomes especially crucial. During the planning for Operation BLIND LOGIC,[110] the military planners realized that they had crossed over into the area that could be considered the realm of the State Department. Attempts to bring the State Department into the planning failed, only allowing information with no specifics on the plan.[111] The State Department thought the military effort to reestablishing the government was amateurish.[112] However, they realized that the military had a plan, whereas the State Department had none.[113] The lesson of interagency coordination rose again during the early days of the occupation of Iraq. It appears that only by close coordination can problems of this nature be resolved in the future.

Role of Civil Affairs Professionals

The next lesson to be extracted from the Panama conflict is the role of the military's Civil Affairs professionals. As there is only one Civil Affairs' Battalion in the Active Army, the Civil Affairs support for Operation PROMOTE LIBERTY came from the U.S. Army Reserve.[114] The first issue was during the

---

[110] Original name for the civil-military operation, later renamed Operation PROMOTE LIBERTY.

[111] Ibid, 21. This is known as "talking around the plan."

[112] Ibid, 38.

[113] Ibid, 38.

[114] Ibid, 8-9.

planning for Operation PROMOTE LIBERTY. SOUTHCOM was supported by the 361st Civil Affairs Brigade, who had fostered a good working relationship with the J-5 since 1983. Although many of the Civil Affairs soldiers had a good familiarity with SOUTHCOM and its missions, it was only for two weeks every year. In an effort to accomplish the required planning on Operation BLIND LOGIC, Civil Affairs officers started to volunteer for thirty-one day planning tours to SOUTHCOM to work on the plan. Although much was accomplished during these planning sessions, it was clear the temporary and rotational nature of their work had adverse effects on continuity of planning. Exasperating the rotational nature of the planning was the constraint caused by compartmentalized classification for the planning of Operations BLUE SPOON and BLIND LOGIC, which prevented them from understanding the details of the combat plan and from going back to their unit and further collaborating on the plan.[115] Clearly, this shortfall requires correction by allowing the Civil Affairs reservist access the compartmentalized plan and allowing a parallel Civil Affairs planning cell at the reservist home station.

Additionally, during the planning for the Operation BLIND LOGIC the assumption had been made that in the event of execution the President would exercise his authority to active selected reserve forces (the 361st) for up to 90 days. The President ultimately did not elect to exercise this power, instead approving a continued volunteer process for 139 days. The soldiers of the 361st could not execute this option due to their civilian employment requirements, leaving responsibilities for the occupation mission to the soldiers on the ground.[116] The lesson here is to ensure that the President understands the assumptions that were made in planning and that the planners have an appropriate branch to execute if their assumption fails.

Occupation Plan vs. Combat Plan

The planners made a poor assumption deciding the Civil Military Operations plan's (BLIND LOGIC) execution separate from the combat plan (BLUE SPOON). Although on the surface this does

---

[115] Ibid, 14-15.

[116] Ibid, 35.

32

not seem to be a significant issue, it became so when other factors were added into the equation. Specifically, the Combatant Commander's change of command from General Woerner to General Thurman added confusion. When General Woerner executed the separation of the two plans he understood both plans and how they integrated together. When General Thurman took command he immediately focused with the combat plan to remove Noriega and not the plan to restore democracy. This is evident as the combat plan (BLUE SPOON) was approved by the JCS by 3 November 1989 after 30 days of intense planning by the SOUTHCOM staff.[117] Where as the Civil-Military Operation plan (OPERATION PROMOTE LIBERTY) was only approved on December 20, 1989 (the first day of the conflict).[118]

This separation of plans created problems in the relationship the US SOUTHCOM staff and the XVIII Corps (Airborne) staff. The lack of agreement between the SOUTHCOM Staff and the JTF-South (XVIII Corps) staff added significantly to this dysfunction. This was due to perceptions that each staff had regarded the significance of OPERATION BLIND LOGIC. Whereas the SOUTHCOM staff worked diligently on the BLIND LOGIC plan, the XVIII Corps planners did not perceive the BLIND LOGIC plan an approved plan. Indeed the XVIII Corps staff thought of the SOUTHCOM Staff as insignificant.[119]

The critical lessons to integrate into future operations are two fold. First, the planning of the combat operation and the follow-on civil-military operation can not be separated. It appears these two elements are now less likely to be separated by time, as many of the elements of the civil-military operations occur in unison with combat operations. Second, the staffs at different levels must

---

[117] Ronald H. Cole, *Operation JUST CAUSE: The Planning and Execution of Joint Operations in Panama, February 1988–January 1990*, (Washington, D.C., Joint History Office, Office of the Chairman of the Joint Chiefs of Staff: 1995), 21-22.

[118] Fishel, 31.

[119] Ibid, 20.

synchronize their plans together. Failure to recognize the scope of the higher headquarters tasks is indefensible.

Unity of Command

The Civil Military Operations Task Force (CMOTF) organized civil military operations within Panama, but it had its own command and control issues. General Woerner had wanted the Commander, CMOTF (COMCMOTF) to be General Officer on his staff responsive to him.[120] The SOUTHCOM J-5 (SCJ5) had the most experience with the BLIND LOGIC plan so he became the COMCMOTF. As the plan ebbed and flowed, the J-5 tried to give the plan away to the US Army South (USARSO). USARSO would have been a great fit, as USARSO possessed a great awareness from being stationed in Panama. USARSO did not object, but additional duties as JTF-Panama kept them from focusing their full attention of the civil-military operation. On 17 December 1989, nearing D-day, the SCJ5 realized that they would have to execute as the CMOTF without handing the plan off to USARSO. Although the J-5 commanded the CMOTF, the preparation and ability to do so was at risk.

Another area of command confusion was task organization of the 361st CA Brigade. Under the PROMOTE LIBERTY Plan the 361st was tasked to staff the CMOTF. In conflict with the PROMOTE LIBERTY Plan, JTF–South had tasked the 361st to establish the Joint Civil Affairs Task Force (JCATF). To add to the confusion, the 361st fell under JTF-South for the first six days of the operation. JTF-South did not acknowledge the CMOTF mission. After six days, the bulk of civil affairs reservists arrived and the SCJ5 had secured control of the CMOTF mission.[121] Although the CMOTF accomplished the mission, a confusing and uncoordinated chain of command structure certainly did not ease any the mission. Clearly, future occupations need a clear and coordinated task organization to aid the unity of command.

---

[120] Ibid, 18.

[121] Ibid, 35.

Much of the success to correct any unity of command issues was due to the efforts of Major

General (MG) Marc Cisneros. The Commander of USARSO and JTF-Panama, MG Cisneros created

other initiatives that aided in the civil-military operations. First, he established the U.S. Forces Liaison

Group (USFLG), a group made up of his Spanish speaking staff officers and others to coordinate and aid

in the development of the Panamanian Public Force (PPF). The PPF was the security apparatus in

Panama designed to replace the Panamanian Defense Force. The PPF consisted of the National Police,

Maritime Services, Air Services, Immigration Services, prison system, Presidential Guard, and the Port

Police.[122] Second, he established the Judicial Liaison Group (JLG) whose function was to get the court

system working, establish a night court system, and liaison between the Panamanian government and US

Government on judicial matters. Only when JLG functions were fully operating could USARSO remove

U.S. forces from their presence patrols and civil-military operations throughout Panama. Major General

Cisneros' initiatives filled the holes in civil-military operations that the COMCMOTF and JCATF both

lacked.[123] MG Cisneros example of leadership simply shows making a proper assessment of the

conditions and positioning forces to control handle the situation. MG Cisneros acted in the void of

guidance to help the Panamanians. Additionally, MG Cisneros' actions provide an excellent example of

transitioning from combat operations to civil military operations.

Military Support Group-Panama

The last lesson from Panama is in the transition to a longer-term effort on behalf of the United

States. On January 17, 1990, the United States Military Support Group-Panama (MSG) was activated.

The MSG's mission was to gain control over the numerous organizations that the United States created to

solve immediate issues after the war, and turn them into long term organizations that supported a partially

structured Panamanian government and a rapidly growing U.S. government presence.[124] The MSG

---

[122] Ibid, 37.

[123] Ibid, 36.

[124] Ibid, 43.

successfully gained control and integrated the USFLG, CMOTF, CATF, PYSOPS, and Military Police. Although the MSG was deactivated one year from its activation, the functions of the MSG continued to support the government of Panama with liaison and an advisory role. The MSG's significance was the transition from a purely military organization responsive to the CINC to an organization that was responsive to and aided the new government of Panama. The MSG offers a possible model of how to conduct the transition from combat to a small scale occupation and finally back to the legitimate government.

Operation Iraqi Freedom

Panama presents a perspective of a limited occupation after a limited war. In contrast, Germany shows a major occupation after a world war. The current occupation of Iraq allows analysis offers a further contrast from both Germany and Panama. Specifically, the occupation of Iraq offers nine lessons which could further aid planners and allow for the creation of doctrine. First, the task organization that was used to conduct the occupation of Iraq presents a different model than both German and Panama. Second, the presence of an insurgency movement in Iraq has added a level of complexity to the occupation. Thirdly, a security structure has been created to protect the Iraqi people. Fourth, the United States and it coalition partners have taken major steps to ensure certain essential services are provided throughout the country. Fifth, the Coalition Provisional Authority has taken steps to establish a democratic form of government. Sixth, efforts have been made to energize and restore the Iraqi economy. Seventh, steps have been taken to remove Saddam Hussein's Baath party. Eighth, the 101st Airborne Division's specific actions offer a model for specific unit conducting the occupation mission. Finally, the creation of the Commander's Emergency Response Program (CERP) is a creative way to apply funds towards occupation and reconstruction efforts.

Organization

The initial organization to handle the occupation after combat operations was a Department of Defense organization called the Office of Reconstruction and Humanitarian Assistance (ORHA), set up in January 20, 2003 to establish "links with the United Nations, specialized agencies and the non-governmental organizations that will play a role in post-war Iraq."[125] Retired Lieutenant General Jay

Garner headed this organization. On 1 May, 2003, President Bush announced the end of combat

operations, after which, on 11 May, 2003, the ORHA transformed into a new organization, the Coalition

Provision Authority (CPA) led by Ambassador Paul Bremer. The mission of the CPA is to temporarily

provide the effective administration of Iraq, to restore conditions of security and stability, and to create

the conditions so that the Iraqi people can determine their own political future.[126] The CPA's mission

includes establishing local and national institutions for a representative government and sustainable

reconstruction and development.[127] The CPA works with the military command in Iraq and the Region.

Central Command (CENTCOM) forces are specifically directed to support the CPA by "deterring

hostilities; maintaining Iraq's territorial integrity and security; searching for, securing and destroying

weapons of mass destruction; and assisting in carrying out Coalition policy generally."[128]

Insurgency

As well as executing the military occupation mission, coalition forces are in the middle of an

insurgency and terrorist activity. The insurgency is believed to consist primarily of remnants of the

Former Regime Loyalists (FRL), in addition to ordinary criminals, Islamic fundamentalists, and external

Arab insurgents.[129] The smallest insurgent faction appears to be the external Arab element. As of August

2003, only 250 of the 9000 detainees in Iraq appeared to be from outside the country.[130] The greatest

concern, however, remains the FRL, whose goal appears to be to break the will of the United States and to

---

[125] "Iraq Reconstruction," <http://www.globalsecurity.org/military/ops/iraq_recon_intro/> [12 JAN 2004].

[126] Coalition Provisional Authority, *Regulation Number 1*, Section 1, (Baghdad, Iraq: 16 May 2003), <http://www.cpa-iraq.org/regulations/REG1.pdf> [12 January 2004].

[127] Ibid, Section 2.

[128] Ibid, Section 3.

[129] "Iraq Insurgency Groups," <http://www.globalsecurity.org/military/ops/iraq _insurgency/> [12 JAN 2004].

[130] Ibid.

hope that the U.S. will prematurely leave before Iraq can become a member of the world community.[131] Insurgent elements have initiated terrorism, including the bombing of the United Nations headquarters on 19 August 2003 and the Jordanian embassy on 17 August 2003[132]

Moreover, the fact that Iraq is a fractured society complicates the problem of insurgency. Two large Muslim religious groups dominate the country, with Shi'a, and Sunni making up 97% of the people practicing religion in the country.[133] This religious divide is laid over a varying ethnic background that also causes fractures within the country. Arabs make up 75% of the population, Kurds 20%, and the remainder consists of Turkomans and Assyrians. Due to the totalitarian rule by Saddam Hussein for the last twenty-four years, the society will undergo a difficult transition to democracy. In addition, Iraq's neighbors do not necessarily support or desire democratic reform and reconstruction in a country that has destabilized the Middle East for over the last decade.[134] Turkey as well has their own open hostility towards certain sectors of the Iraqi population.[135]

The situation in Iraq contrast dramatically with Germany and Panama. Germany had very little insurgency after the war and resistance efforts in Panama were mopped rather quickly.[136] The significant lesson is that the counterinsurgency/security mission and the civil-military operations mission are difficult enough when conducted separately, but the difficulties are further amplified when conducted together.

---

[131] Ibid.

[132] Andrew England, "Explosion rocks Jordanian Embassy in Iraq, kills at least 11", Seattle Times, August 8, 2003., <http://seattletimes.nwsource.com/html/nationworld/2001406000_webiraqexplosion07.html> [12 Jan 2004].

[133] "Religious Structures," <http://www.globalsecurity.org/military/world/iraq/religion.htm> [12 Jan 2004]

[134] "President Bush Discusses Freedom in Iraq and Middle East," Remarks by the President at the 20th Anniversary of the National Endowment for Democracy, United States Chamber of Commerce, 6 November 2003, Washington, D.C., < http://www.whitehouse.gov/news/releases/2003/11/20031106-2.html> [12 Jan 2004].

[135] Turkey's ongoing dispute with the Kurds as noted in, "Bush Reassures Turkey on Kurds," washingtontimes.com, 28 Jan 2004, <http://washingtontimes.com/upi-breaking/20040128-033953-6801r.htm> [28 Jan 2004]

[136] As Cole notes, Looting took place on 20 Dec 1989, which initiated greater civil affairs participation, 52. Fishel attributes this to the changes in plan, separating the combat plan from the civil-military plan, 31. The last PDF surrendered on 25 December 1989, Cole, 65.

Planners of future occupations should consider the impacts that possible insurgency may have on the completion of occupation tasks.

Security

The CPA has specifically focused their efforts in four areas: security, essential services, restoration of government, and economy.[137] In the first area of security, there are three components consisting of the Iraqi Security Forces, the Iraqi courts, and the Prison system. The first is the Iraqi Security Forces created to transition to and eventually provide the security for the country of Iraq. The Iraqi Security Forces consist of the National Defense Forces, Border Police, Facilities Protection services, and the Iraqi Police. Currently, there are over 200,000 Iraqis integrated into the security structure of their country. Initial tasks were to create a new Ministry of Defense and Military Industrialization, a new Iraqi National Defense Force, and a new Iraqi Army of 1000 trained soldiers, with thousands more awaiting training.[138] The defense force includes the Iraqi Civil Defense Corps, which integrates into and works with coalition military forces.

Another force ready in training and transitioning to full responsibilities in Iraq is the Border Police. Currently at full strength, the Border Police is responsible for the security of the Iraqi Borders.[139] The Facilities Protection service is responsible for securing critical areas of the infrastructure, including banks, hospitals, power stations, and oil and gas production facilities. General security and law enforcement falls under the responsibility of the Iraqi Police forces. U.S. and Coalition forces have directed training and assisted in the formation of all of these units.[140]

---

[137] Iraq Weekly Update, Joint Staff/Coalition Provisional Authority, 09 Jan 2004 <http://www.globalsecurity.org/ wmd/library/news/iraq/2004/01/iraq-weekly-js-cpa-20040109.pdf> [12 JAN 2004]. This presentation shows economic, oil, education, health care, security, governance, and power measures of effectiveness and statistics.

[138] Ibid.

[139] Ibid

[140] "Iraqi Military Reconstruction," <http://www.globalsecurity.org/military/world/iraq/iraq-corps.htm> [12 JAN 2004].

The CPA's second focus in security is the new Iraqi court system. The CPA has presided over the reestablishment of over 500 courts with over 600 judges throughout Iraq.[141] The priority of the CPA's efforts has been to eliminate the corruption and favoritism that was associated with justice in pre-invasion Iraq.[142] In some cases, the CPA removed ex-Baathist as was permissible in international law.[143] Additionally, the U.S. appointed Iraqi Governing Council has set up an Iraqi Special Tribunal.[144]

The CPA's final focus area in security is the prison system. Before the overthrow of the Baathists regime, the prisons failed to meet any international human rights standards.[145] Now there are over 4000 beds meeting international standards.[146]

The security efforts in Iraq are not unprecedented. In Panama, Major General Cisneros initiatives also set up the three pillars of security, a security force, judicial system, and a penal system. Similarly in Germany, the Unites States established the constabulary force to aid in security and train new German security forces in addition to military tribunals to serve as a temporary court system until the german reestablished their courts.[147] The security issues will occur every time an occupation occurs and they must be appropriately planned for.

Essential Services

The second area that the CPA is focused on is the reestablishment of essential services. The CPA breaks the essential services down into six sub-areas to track more effectively: electricity, telecommunications, health care, education, water, and oil.

---

[141] John D. Banusiewicz, " Bremer: 'Future of Hope' in Iraq includes Justice," *Armed Forces Information Service*, November 14 2003, <http://www.defenselink.mil/news/Nov2003/n11142003_200311147.html> [12 JAN 2004].

[142] Ibid.

[143] GC, Art. 54.

[144] "Building Justice," < http://www.cpa-iraq.org/security/justice.html> [12 Jan 2004].

[145] Ibid.

[146] Ibid.

[147] Zink, 108, 125.

Electricity

The United States has received much criticism for failing to provide electricity in a reasonable amount of time.[148] Actually, the electrical situation in Iraq was in a woeful state of disrepair before the U.S. occupation, due to poor investment in infrastructure, sanctions, and because only relatively minor repairs occurred after the first Gulf War.[149] Looting and sabotage after the war further deteriorated the electrical infrastructure. The CPA has set up goals to ensure it restores the electrical system and prepares for future demands. The CPA monitors the electrical situation in Iraq daily and although the electrical supply has not met the electrical demands the goal to meet the increased demand for the summer of 2004 is on schedule. The CPA has also pushed hard on electrical issues to ensure that repairs and money are dedicated toward their goals.[150] In comparison to Germany, the reliance on electricity is much more prevalent today than in was in 1945. The reconstruction of Iraq represents a new era reliant on electrical support to sustain the community and is an excellent example of the needs in future occupations.

Telecommunications

Another area that is in dire need of repair is the telecommunication's sector. Prior to the war telecommunication services were privileges for the selected few. The CPA has now initiated new contracts to aid in country wide connectivity. The CPA is emplacing fiber-optic links to meet the initial countrywide need. International service has been restored with Intelsat satellite equipment.[151] In 2004, telecommunications is a priority as it reestablishes Iraq with the world and in turn financial networks, business and education opportunities, information services, and health care systems.

---

[148] Alissa J. Rubin, "U.S. Struggles in Quicksand of Iraq," *Los Angeles Times*, May 5 2003, sec. A, p. 1. Her commentary is not alone. In the aftermath of the war (combat phase) most of the news services concentrated on the difficulties and challenges the United States faced as an occupation force.

[149] Gerry J. Gilmore, "'Incredible Progress' Made Restoring Iraq's Infrastructure, Officials Say," *American Forces Information Services*, July 7 2003. <http://www.defenselink.mil/news/Jul2003/n07072003_200307075.html> [12 JAN 2004].

[150] Iraq Weekly Update, Joint Staff/Coalition Provisional Authority, 09 Jan 2004

[151] "Telecoms," <http://www.cpa-iraq.org/essential_services/telecoms.html> [12 JAN 2004].

Health Care

One of the greatest successes comes in the area of health care. Only $16 million was spent on health care under the Saddam Hussein's regime, causing the neglect of most individuals. The most telling figure was an infant mortality rate of 1 in 10,[152] which places Iraq as the country with the highest infant mortality rate in western Asia. Additionally, as a collateral consequence of the war, looting eliminated most hospitals supplies and equipment. Spending on health care is twenty-six times what was spent under the old regime. All 240 Iraqi hospitals and over 1200 clinics have been reopened. Doctors pay has increased eight times over their previous pre-war pay. Over 22 million immunizations have been given since the end of the war and UNICEF started vitamin distribution in January 2004. Furthermore, Iraq now has a renewed emphasis on preventive medicine procedures and disease management.[153] The health care efforts demonstrated in Iraq has set the example for future occupations to follow.

Education

In the realm of education, the great hurdle to overcome was the indoctrination which consisted of praising Saddam Hussein. In order to accomplish this every textbook had to be replaced, and teachers had to be retrained on new teaching methods. By the end of the 2004 school year, the CPA will have distributed 72 million new textbooks. Additionally, pay has increased for teachers to 12 to 25 times their former salaries.[154] As of October 2003, the universities, technical institutes, and colleges were reopened and 1500 elementary schools had been renewed. These efforts show a regard for the law[155] and mirror the efforts in Germany after WWII. In Germany, they were challenged to keep the children occupied, finding and screening teachers, and locating suitable buildings for schools.[156]

---

[152] United Nations Statistical database, <http://millenniumindicators.un.org/unsd/mi/mi_goals.asp> [12 Feb 2004]. This rate is 20 times higher than most western governments, and compares readily to most central African states.

[153] Iraq Weekly Update, Joint Staff/Coalition Provisional Authority, 09 Jan 2004

[154] Iraq Weekly Update, Joint Staff/Coalition Provisional Authority, 09 Jan 2004

[155] GC, Art. 50.

[156] Ziemke, 358. Average age of the teachers in Munich was 57 and the student-teacher ratio was 89 to 1.

Water

Water resources mirror the substandard state of the electrical infrastructure. Pump stations and generators are 20-30 years old and were poorly maintained for the last ten years. Moreover, Iraq's water distribution system is one of the most complex systems in the world. The CPA is conducting an extensive program clearing irrigation canals and water transportation until the system is working at reasonable levels.[157] Quartermaster unit's reverse osmosis water purification has had a major effect in areas where the water system has failed.[158] Additionally, Iraqi engineers have been training with the Army Corps of Engineers in California to test new models for the Tigris–Euphrates water system.[159] Units have energized the Iraqi population to find better methods to improve their water supply issues.[160] The supply of suitable water will continued to challenge future occupation forces.

Oil

The last essential service is Iraqi's most lucrative asset, oil. Although the Coalition forces were very conscious of the dangers to the oil fields during the war and realized that they needed preserve the field with minimal damage, thefts from looting after the war were widespread. Efforts to increase the production of oil back to pre-Gulf War capacity is the goal for the end of 2004. The sale of the oil is critical to cover Iraq's reconstruction costs. To this end, LOGPAC contracts have been put in place to assist in the repair of the oil fields. Immediately following the war, U.S. forces patrolled the oil fields and pipelines. As of January 2004 Iraqi Force Protection services took over the security for these areas.[161]

---

[157] Iraq Weekly Update, Joint Staff/Coalition Provisional Authority, 09 Jan 2004

[158] Cpl. Jeff Hawk, "Water Flows from the Desert," *USMC News*, April 15 2003. <http://www.globalsecurity.org/wmd/library/news/iraq/2003/iraq-030415-usmc01.htm> [12 JAN 2004].

[159] "Water Resources," <http://www.cpa-iraq.org/essential_services/water-management.html> [12 JAN 2004].

[160] United States Central Command, "Conference Seeks Ways to Improve Iraq's Water Supply," *News Release*, January 21 2004, Release Number 04-01-52. <http://www.centcom.mil/CENTCOMNews/release_list.asp> [23 JAN 2004].

[161] Jackie Spinner, "Iraqi Oil Gets Its Own Police Force," *Washington Post*, 17 January 2004, sec. E, p. 1, <http://www.washingtonpost.com/ac2/wp-dyn/A23664-2004Jan16> [24 Jan 2004]. Also see Charles Recknegel, "Iraq: Oil Production Strengthens But Remains Problematic," Radio Free Europe/Radio Liberty, 31 July 2003, <http://www.globalsecurity.org/wmd/library/news/iraq/2003/07/iraq-030731-rfel-151445.htm> [24 Jan 2004]. Additionally, on

The United States' emphasis on oil may initially appear duplicitous, only focused on oil for the benefit of the United States. However, the CPA understands that oil is the key to Iraq's economy and the sooner the oil flows to bring in money the better will be Iraq's economy and people. This is a lesson learned in contrast to Germany and a change from the reparations that Germany was forced to pay immediately to Russia and France.

Government

The next specified area that the CPA is developing is the Iraqi Government. Approved by the United Nations, 25 representatives were selected to form the Iraqi Governing Council (IGC). Broadly representing the Iraqi people, this council serves two purposes. The first purpose is to shorten the duration of the CPA's interim administration so that the Iraqi people can elect and administer a government with a viable constitution. To this end, it is important that the Iraqis see a timeline with specific events leading restoration of sovereignty. Critical in this process is the agreement upon the Iraqi Fundamental Law that the future Constitution will be based upon. Secondly, the IGC represents Iraq internationally and to international organizations. Since the formation of the IGC, it has represented Iraq to the UN General Assembly, the Arab League, the World Bank and IMF and the Organization of the Islamic Conference Summit. This representation will include reopening Iraqi embassies around the world.[162]

At the local government level, Iraqis are now conducting daily operations. A majority of the towns and cities have functioning local governments. The CPA holds up Baghdad as the example for local representative based government. "In each of Baghdad's 88 neighborhoods, citizens have freely selected representatives for local governing councils. They, in turn, choose members of 9 District

---

the Global Security website, they present all the week update briefings that show oil production and goals, <http://www.globalsecurity.org/wmd/library/news/iraq/2004/01/iraq-weekly-js-cpa-20040109.pdf> [12 Jan 2004].

[162] Associated Press, "Iraq Council Members Meet With U.N," *Fox News Channel*, July 22, 2003, <http://www.foxnews.com/story/0,2933,92589,00.html> [24 Jan 2004].

Councils and a 37-member City Council. All told, over 800 democratically selected Council Members are now hard at work serving their fellow citizens."[163]

Economy

The last specific focus area for the CPA is the economy. Much effort has been expended in erasing old corrupt methods while trying to increase growth in the economy. In the public sector, all transactions and budgeting is now in the open for all to see. The CPA has overhauled commercial laws to prevent corruption. Additionally, the CPA has enacted laws to ensure equal pay for equal work. In the private sector the CPA has encouraged the establishment of goals to increase wealth and income and provide for a stable government. Moreover, they focused efforts on assisting state-operated firms to resume normal operations and transition into the private sector. Development of foreign investment and businesses has and will lead to further economic growth. Banks have expanded their transactions to the international level.[164]

Debaathification

Saddam Hussein and his Baath Party caused the Iraqi people severe hardships which require the removal of their imprint on society. Two primary tasks are associated with the debaathification of Iraq. The first task is the removal of the plethora of images and views of Saddam Hussein etched into the Iraqi infrastructure and culture. Saddam Hussein's widespread image was removed from the physical structures throughout Iraq. As mentioned before, the writing of textbooks has reinforced debaathification of Iraq. Additionally, Saddam Hussein's image was erased from the Iraqi currency. In many ways the elimination of the Baath party is similar to the efforts to rid Germany of the Nazi Party after WWII. Like the Nazi party, the Baath party had a huge membership of 2.5 million people intertwined with every part of the society. Many had duplicitous reasons for joining. Not all members were Saddam loyalists, but

---

[163] "Representative Government at the local level," <http://www.cpa-iraq.org/government/local_level.html> [12 JAN 2004].

[164] "Economy," <http://www.cpa-iraq.org/economy.html> [12 JAN 2004].

joined the party to fulfill their ambitions, to provide protection to themselves and their family, or to avoid punishment for disloyalty. The hard question is what to do with this percentage of the population. Some would fire them from their jobs to demonstrate justice, which could have a negative effect by pushing the ex-Baathists and their families to the side of the insurgents. The impact of otherwise firing such a great number of people could not only have a bad effect on security, but would hurt the reconstruction effort, as many of these Baath Party members were in critical positions in society. In an effort to control the impact some Coalition units have administered ex-Baath denunciations of the Baath party by voluntary loyalty oaths [165]

101st Airborne Division (Air Assault)

Interestingly, the 101st Airborne Division has set the standard for the rest of the theater in many of the occupation tasks they have executed. Creatively, they have restored trade with Syria and initiated taxes to support the customs forces required to man the crossing sites. The 101st also set up an employment agency to assist in the reemployment of out of work military officers. In many cases, the CPA has followed the 101st's actions. As the CPA civilian coordinators have increased their presence in the 101st's region, the 101st realized that they still had the manpower and worked with the CPA to accomplish joint goals.[166]

Commander's Emergency Response Program

MG Petraeus said, "Money is ammunition."[167] The Commander's Emergency Response Program (CERP) is a method of providing governmental appropriations directly to tactical units for meeting the emergency needs for the local Iraqi population. The initial money for this program was captured U.S. dollars from the Iraqi regime's hidden coffers, which allowed units to meet the urgent humanitarian needs of the populace. Eventually, appropriated funds were approved for the same purpose. The benefits in

---

[165] United States Central Command, "120 Baathists Renounce Political Party," *News Release*, January 20 2004, Release Number 04-01-50, <http://www.centcom.mil/CENTCOMNews/release_list.asp> [23 JAN 2004]

[166] Michael R. Gordon, "101st Airborne Scores Success in northern Iraq," *New York Times*, 4 Sept 2003, Sec. A, p. 8.

[167] Gordon, p. 8.

Iraq were remarkable. Purchases of air conditioners, generators, building materials, and road construction materials and equipment all went to the benefit of the Iraqi people. As of mid-October 2003, the 101st completed over 3600 CERP projects at a cost of 28 million dollars, a one-third of the total CERP activity in Iraq.[168]

Summary

This analysis has shown the lessons learned from the application of two past occupations and of one ongoing. The occupation of Germany, pre-1949 Geneva protocol, shows application without the mandate of the current law. It is also reflective of an occupation of a huge magnitude after a completely devastating war, including restoration of the German infrastructure, a reestablishment of the government, the repatriation of millions of displaced people, and the dissolving of a dangerous ideology. In contrast, Panama shows an occupation after a limited war and a country with only slight damage to the infrastructure. Currently, Iraq offers another model of a large occupation overlaid on a multiethnic, religiously divisive country repressed by more than 20 years of totalitarian rule.

Most importantly these occupations further build a model for occupation doctrine. These occupations reveal issues regarding organizational structures, treatment of international law, the importance of planning and having an objective, the importance of the interagency team, command and control issues, the role and use of the soldiers, establishment of government, and the removal of dangerous ideologies. All of theses are common trends that permeate all the occupations.

In Chapter 2, this monograph established, based on international law, the minimum standard for all occupation. This chapter has added specific tasks conducted in an occupation, which can further add to doctrine. The law establishes the framework for doctrine and the application fills in the possible gaps.

---

[168] Mark Martins, "No Small Change of Soldiering: The Commander's Emergency Response Program (CERP) in Iraq and Afghanistan," *Army Lawyer*, February 2004, 8.

CHAPTER 4

DOCTRINE

Introduction

Joint Publication 1-02, Dictionary for Military and Associated Terms defines doctrine as

"[f]undamental principles by which the military forces or elements thereof guide their actions in support

of national objectives. It is authoritative but requires judgment in application."[169] The Army definition

amplifies and provides more clarity, saying, it "is the concise expression of how Army forces contribute

to unified action in campaigns, major operations, battles, and engagements...facilitates communication

among soldiers no matter where they serve...must be well known and commonly understood."[170]

Military doctrine appears expansive at first glance, encompassing thousands of documents on areas of

military art and science. Accordingly, it is appropriate to assume that doctrine should include basic

principles of a military occupation. In this chapter the paper will review current doctrine and past

doctrine offering guidance on military occupation and determine if doctrine meets the criteria set forth

from the law and history.

Current Doctrine

An examination of current doctrine begins with reviewing joint publications to determine what, if

any, joint doctrine is available, followed by a similar examination of Army doctrine. The review will

examine doctrine from general to specific terms, and will consider Joint Publications (JP) *3-0, Doctrine*

for Joint Operations; 3-07 Joint Doctrine for Military Operations Other than War, and 3-57 Joint

Doctrine for Civil-Military Operations as well as *Field Manuals (FM) 3-0, Operations; 3-07, Stability*

and Support Operations; 41-10, Civil Affairs Operations, and *27-10 Law of Land Warfare.*

---

[169] Department of Defense, *Joint Publication 1-02, Dictionary for Military and Associated Terms*, Headquarters, Joint Chiefs of Staff, 17 December 2003, <http://www.dtic.mil/doctrine/jel/new_pubs/jp1_02.pdf> [24 JAN 2004]

[170] Department of the Army, *Field Manual 3.0 Operations*, Headquarters, Department of the Army, Washington, D.C., June 2001, Chapter 1, 14.

Joint Doctrine

The first document to be examined is *JP 3-0 Operations*.[171] *Joint Publication 3-0* says nothing about the mission of occupation, and makes only slight reference to military government. In referring to termination criteria, in strategic context, *JP 3-0* states that military government should be considered in the political exploitation of the completed military action. Additionally, *JP 3-0* describes the necessity for early planning, liaison, and coordination at the national and theater level between diplomatic, military, and political leadership prior to conducting these operations.[172] Being a very broad document, *JP 3.0*, does frame the scope of military operations from war to military operations other than war (MOOTW),[173] but does not address the mission of occupation.

Like *JP 3-0, JP 3-07, Joint Doctrine for Military Operations Other than War*, also does not specifically refer to the mission of occupation. Unlike *JP 3-0, JP 3-07* does not even reference military government. The manual does briefly describe post-conflict operations in the context of transition from wartime activities, and discusses the possible need to realign forces as missions change as well as the possibility that military forces may be in the support role to other agencies. Unfortunately, it offers tasks only in generalities.[174] Like *JP 3-0, JP 3-07* may be deferring the details of military occupation doctrine for a more specific manual.

JP 3-57, Joint Doctrine for Civil-Military Operations and *JP 3-57.1, Joint Doctrine for Civil Affairs* appears to offer more specifics on military occupation. *Joint Publication 3-57* provides a framework what an occupation is, although it avoids the word occupation and refers instead to a civil administration, under the task of support to civil operations. The manual breaks down civil

---

[171] Department of Defense, *Joint Publication 3-0 Doctrine for Joint Operations*, Headquarters, Joint Chiefs of Staff, Washington D.C., 10 September 2001.

[172] *JP 3-0*, I 12.

[173] *JP 3-0*, I 2.

[174] *JP 3-07*, IV 11-12. In states potential tasks as 1) transition to civil authorities, 2) support to truce negotiations, 3) Civil Affairs support to reestablish a civil government, 4) Psychological operations to foster continued peaceful relations, and 5) Continuing logistic support from engineering and transportation units.

administration further into two parts: civil administration in friendly territory, and civil administration in enemy territory. The manual also discusses who will provide civil administration, asserting that this is not a military decision and that the military is generally in a support effort. At the same time, the manual also realizes that the military is the only element that can stabilize the situation in order to execute a civil administration. Finally, the document notes that planning must occur early and be integrated with other operations and with other agencies.[175] Beyond this informality, it offers little to aid in planning or executing an occupation.

Joint Publication 3-57.1 offers slightly more detail than *JP 3-57*. It makes reference to the applicable international law, including a glancing reference to the Geneva and Hague Regualtions referenced in Chapter 1 of this monograph. It goes on to state however, that civil administration is the responsibility of the civil affairs community.[176] The manual further elaborates that the President is the only one to authorize a civil administration. Like *JP 3-57*, it makes the distinction between civil administration in friendly territory and civil administration in hostile or occupied territory. In a friendly territory it states the importance of coordination with the Host Nation. In occupied territory, *JP 3-57.1* describes the importance of the parameters set by international law. Finally, *JP 3-57.1* states the role of and analysis required by the Joint Force Commander when the military is in control of the territory.[177]

Both *JP 3-57* and *JP 3-57.1* avoid the term and only touch upon the potential complexities associated with mission of occupation. The introduction of Joint Doctrine has not added much to occupation doctrine.

---

[175] Department of Defense, *Joint Publication 3-57 Joint Doctrine for Civil-Military Operations*, Headquarters, Joint Chiefs of Staff, Washington D.C., 8 Feb 2001, I 17-20.

[176] Department of Defense, *Joint Publication 3-57.1 Joint Doctrine for Civil Affairs*, Headquarters, Joint Chiefs of Staff, Washington D.C., 14 April 2003, I 9.

[177] *JP 3-57.1*, I 10.

Army Doctrine

The Army's bedrock of operational doctrine is *Field Manual 3-0, Operations.*[178] Although *FM 3-0* states nothing about an occupation, or civil administration, or military government it does offer the parameter of full spectrum operations to provide a framework for the mission of occupation. The inference could easily be made that the occupation mission should fall under the stability and support range of full spectrum operations. However, further research into *Field Manual 3-07, Stability and Support Operations* does not refer to the occupation mission.[179] The most beneficial Army Manual is *Field Manual 41-10 Civil Affairs Operations. Field Manual 41-10* marks the separation between civil administration in friendly territory and civil administration in occupied territory. In both cases *FM 41-10* offers broad guidance. For friendly territory, *FM 41-10* reiterates some of the same guidance as the *JP3-57.1.* Additionally, the manual stresses the importance of non-governmental organizations (NGOs) and international organizations and the importance of the civil-military relationship.[180] For occupied territory it offers a little more guidance than either *JP 3-57* or *JP 3-57.1.* It makes the distinction that the civil administration in occupied territory is imposed by force. Second, it notes a need for a goal to create an effective government. Lastly, it offers three methods for executing an occupation. The first keeps the existing government in place; the second selectively removes and replaces suspect personnel; and the third creates a completely new government. Ultimately, the Army doctrine relevant to is only little more comprehensive than the Joint doctrine. It also needs noted that *FM 41-10* individually covers some of the tasks outlined in Chapters 2 and 3 of this monograph.[181]

---

[178] *FM 3-0*, Chapter 1, 15.

[179] Department of the Army, *Field Manual 3-07 Stability and Support Operations*, Headquarters, Department of the Army, Washington, D.C., 20 February 2003.

[180] Department of the Army, *Field Manual 41-10 Civil Affairs Operations*, Headquarters, Department of the Army, Washington, D.C., February 2000, Chapter 2, 29-30.

[181] *FM 41-10* is a very thorough document and covers the structure and capabilities of the U.S. Army's Civil Affairs units. Many of the tasks that this monograph derives from the law and historical case studies can be found *individually* in FM 41-10, but there is no overarching structure in FM 41-10 that brings these tasks together to apply to the specific mission of occupation. Emphasis is mine.

Field Manual 27-10, The Law of Land Warfare should also be examined. This document was created after World War II and the approval of the Geneva conventions of 1949. *Field Manual 27-10* offers the applicable international law and the United States' interpretation of those laws. Chapter 6 is dedicated towards occupation and outlines the law very well. However, the manual focuses on the law and does not describe how to apply that law on the battlefield or occupied territory.[182] Nonetheless, there are two benefits in *FM 27-10*. It is grounded in the law and makes specific references throughout the manual to the Geneva and Hague protocols, which were approved out of the aftermath of World War II. Additionally, it offers the Army interpretation of those international laws providing guidance on what tasks must be done. Indeed, *FM 27-10* is the only current doctrine that offers any substantive information on the required tasks to execute in an occupation. Conversely, none, including *FM 27-10*, of the current doctrine presents substantive guidance on how to execute an occupation. Obviously, there are glaring deficiencies in current occupation doctrine. Other than *FM 27-10*, current doctrine offers nothing on how to conduct an occupation.

Past Doctrine

The most significant occupation examined in this monograph is post-World War II Germany and from that occupation came many examples of relevant doctrine. Especially when compared with current doctrine on occupation, two documents from the World War II era offer outstanding examples of how occupation should be executed. First, *FM 27-5, Civil Affairs Military Governance* originally published in 1940. The scope of *FM 27-5* differs dramatically from its current doctrinal counterparts.[183] *Field Manual 27-5* specifically laid out the scope and purpose of civil affairs and military government activities, organization, personnel, operations orders, proclamation, and tribunals. Where current doctrine only

---

[182] Department of the Army, *Field Manual 27-10 The Law of Land Warfare*, Headquarters, Department of the Army, Washington, D.C., July 1956, 138-164.

[183] In 1958, *FM 41-5, Joint Manual of Civil Affairs/Military Government* superceded and removed some of the detail that *FM 27-5* had. In 1962, *FM 41-10 Civil Affairs Operations* replaced *FM 41-5* and there was further removal of the specifics for military government. By the next revision in 1969, military government became even further indistinct.

starts to sketch the concept of what an occupation is, *FM 27-5* demonstrates the application of legally required occupation tasks on the battlefield including medical care, government, administration, and security. Unlike the lack of current doctrine on occupation, *Field Manual 27-5* provided one reference source for anyone needing information on the conduct of an occupation.[184] *Field Manual 27-5* was superceded by *FM 41-10 Civil Affairs,* provided "procedural and doctrinal framework within which the Army could conduct civil affairs and military government should the need arise."[185] The current *FM 41-10* is certainly not the procedural and doctrinal framework for occupation. However, the earlier version still has worth today.

The second doctrinal document is the *Handbook for Military Government in Germany* written by the German Country Unit in 1944,[186] which provided complete guidance and direction for the military government soldier on the battlefield. Moreover, the very existence of this handbook demonstrates that the planners and military government soldiers had completely thought through their upcoming actions. The *Handbook for Military Government in Germany* is a specific application of the principles outlined in *FM 27-5,* and was the specific resource for the occupation in Germany. The *Handbook* provided the framework for execution and the training for military government soldiers, and set forth policy and provided the basic documents such as proclamations, law, ordinances applicable for every military governance officer in Germany.[187]

Summary

Field Manual 27-5 and the *Handbook* produced for Germany were products that discussed what to do and how to do it. However, a quick review of current doctrine on occupations shows a disturbing

---

[184] Departments of the Army and Navy, *Field Manual 27-5 Civil Affairs Military Government*, Washington D.C., 14 OCT 1947.

[185] Ziemke, vi.

[186] Supreme Headquarters Allied Expeditionary Force, *Handbook for Military Government in Germany,* December 1944, <http://www-cgsc.army.mil/carl/resources/books.asp#military> [12 JAN 2004].

[187] The Handbook for Military Government in Germany.

lack of guidance. Currently, the military has no more than a few pages on the subject. As such, the civil affairs and military communities have grown and adjusted into an environment based on Cold War thinking, which conjectured military occupation would never again take place, and had grown away from the possibility of conducting an occupation. It is time to reconsider this lack of doctrine and consider the law, history, and past doctrine offer a method to resolve this problem.

CHAPTER 5

CONCLUSIONS AND RECOMMENDATIONS

As demonstrated in Chapter 4, there is a substantial lack of doctrine on occupation. This takes on incredible importance because combat victory today may well not achieve the strategic goals set by the President and the Secretary of Defense. Only winning the peace will fulfill those goals. More importantly, this monograph has outlined tasks that could readily form current doctrine. Chapter 2 has outlined the international law requirements that must be fulfilled. Chapter 3 has shown major lessons of past occupations that could benefit future planners. Chapter 4 has shown that there was occupation doctrine and that it was a benefit to the Army during the occupation of Germany.

Additionally, Chapters 2 and 3 show trends and relationships that offer a rudimentary model that could assist planners and operators in the next occupation. The model consists of two parts. First, there are the essential tasks that the law and experience dictate. Second, there are the occupational considerations which describe characteristic of successful occupations.

Of course the essential tasks are focused around the five essential tasks from The Hague and Geneva Conventions as outlined in Chapter 2. As a quick review these five essential tasks are: (1) restore and ensure public order and safety, (2) provide medical care, supplies and subsistence, (3) ensure the care and education of children, (4) respect private property and properly manage public property, and (5) provide for the security of the occupying force to facilitate mission accomplishment. Each of these essential tasks has implied tasks, dictated by the law, that support them directly.

However, there are four additional essential tasks that the lessons from the case studies have directed. These tasks are: (1) the establishment of a new government, (2) the reestablishment of essential services, (3) reestablishment of the economy, (4) and removal of dangerous ideologies. Each one of these will be addressed individually (see Figure 2).

One critical task that will routinely occur is the establishment of a new government. Obviously, this is a by product of an invasion and occupation. Therefore, the objectionable government must be replaced or at a minimum the influencing official need to be replaced. In Germany, the government had collapsed Allied forces surged into Germany. Local government was subsequently re-established first at the local level and slowly expanded to the national level. In Panama with the removal of Manuel Noriega and the fall of his power source, the PDF left a void in government responsibilities. A new leader was emplaced, and the U.S. assisted in the setting up of government actions, such as security and emergency services. In Iraq, the ruling government disintegrated after the fall of Baghdad. The U.S. assisted in the establishment of local leaders, a governing council, and most recently in the approval of an interim constitution.

The second task is that of essential services. The CPA correctly identified essential services that in their absence or failure would cause tremendous hardship on the inhabitant and the occupiers. In Iraq, the CPA identified electricity, telecommunications, health care, education, water, and oil. In the case of health care and education, they are already essential tasks that are dictated by the law. Without these essential services the occupation and reconstruction would be severely hampered.

Another task that the law does directly address but should be considered an essential task is the restoration of the economy. The restoration of the economy infuses money into the hands of people, allowing them to provide for themselves and buying goods and services, which places more money in the society, which causes businesses to grow, creating work and thus more money in the community. The CPA has focused their effort to restore Iraq's oil capability, financial markets, accounting procedures, and market reforms.

The last essential task that should be included is the removal of dangerous ideologies. In Germany it was Nazism and in Iraq it was Saddam Hussein and his Baath Party. This will routinely occur in an occupation since the reasons that led up to the invasion and removal were reasons that the United States took issue with. If the ideologies are powerful, they filtered through all aspects of society, into the education system, business practices, local government, and religious practices. An understanding of the ideology and the integration within society is then necessary in order to properly eradicate the ideology's impact. Much like Germany and Iraq, this must be balanced with the need for further restoration of the country. A required vetted process should be implemented to ensure the removal of this ideology is balanced with retribution, punishment, and restoration of the society. As with an objectionable government, dangerous ideologies tend to be a collateral reason for invasion and the subsequent occupation and will have to be dealt with by occupation forces.

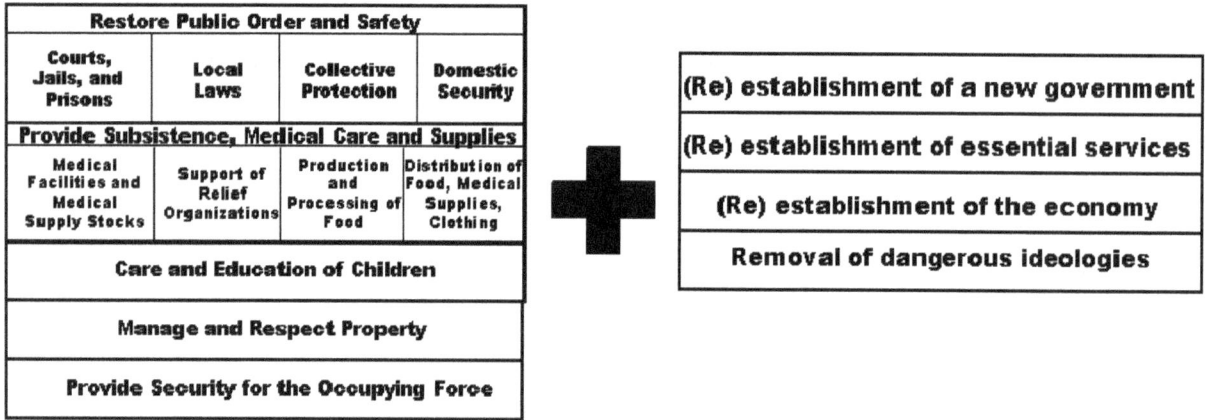

Figure 2, Essential tasks based on law and case analysis

The lessons from the case studies also show us considerations for occupation. In contrast to the essential tasks that state what must be done, these occupational considerations describe characteristics for a successful occupation. These considerations are critical in planning and in execution; disregarding them ensures increased risk. From the lessons of history, there are ten tenets that are revealed. These considerations have been a reoccurring theme throughout the case studies. These tenets are: (1)

organization, (2) preparation, (3) objective, (4) unity of command, (5) integration with combat operations, (6) role of civil affairs, (7) interagency, (8) economy of force, and (9) financial ability (see Figure 3).

- **Organization**
- **Preparation**
- **Objective**
- **Unity of command**
- **Integration with combat operations**
- **Role of civil affairs**
- **Interagency**
- **Economy of force**
- **Financial ability**

Figure 3, Considerations for occupations

The first consideration is that of organization. This monograph has presented three different organization structures for occupation. In all three cases they started as another structure and eventually transformed into the final organization. Each transformation was for different reasons. In Germany, the consolidation into OMGUS was primarily done to prevent duplication of effort. In Panama the MSG was created to assist the Panamanian Government over the long term. In Iraq, the CPA was established after what appears to be a failure to acknowledge the magnitude of the occupation. One could make the assumption that these changes were due to faulting planning, but one could also draw the lesson that there is a natural shift necessary in the organization to better facilitate command and control and occupational tasks. For example, the starting organization is responsible for the initial international law mandated occupation tasks or for occupation tasks while still in an area under conflict. The transition could occur as the activities and conditions become more stable. Not that any of these models were perfect, but all three offered models for future use. The consideration from the analysis of these organizational structures is the importance of the early creation of an organization and the understanding that it will transform as the occupation grows.

The second consideration is that of preparation. The model for preparation should be the actions taken prior to the occupation in Germany. The reason the United States preparation was so successful in Germany was three-fold: 1) establishing a military governance school; 2) training military government soldiers; and 3) publishing doctrine for their specific missions and areas.

The third area for consideration is the importance of a clear objective established for the occupation. As was demonstrated in WWII, there was much ado caused by the position presented in the Morgenthau plan. If the Morgenthau plan was going to set the objectives for the occupation then the occupation forces actions would have been completely different than if they were to fully restore Germany. In one case they would have forced the German people into an agrarian existence, whereas the other regenerated the German people and society without the Nazi dogma. This is also reflected in the occupation of Iraq. As numerous sources have stated, the last priority for the Bush administration was the occupation following the overthrow of Saddam Hussein and the Baath party.[188] Without a clear objective the occupation is left floundering with no discernable direction. The situation in Iraq was eventually corrected with the CPA and the establishment of its measures of effectiveness.

One of the nine principles of war, unity of command, is the fourth area of consideration. The intent here is not to restate this principle, but to reemphasize its importance in the transition from combat to occupation. Panama offers a great lesson when the unity of command was not adhered to, as a Civil-military command was created and not resourced or synchronized with other efforts going on in the area of operations. Ultimately, MG Cisneros' leadership and vision filled the void.

The fifth area for consideration is the integration of the occupation with combat operations. The occupation plan must be integrated with the combat plan. As in Panama, the separation of the two caused

---

[188] James Fallows, "Blind into Baghdad," Atlantic Monthly, January/February, 2004, 52-74.

a lack of staff synchronization and cooperation as the plans did not support each other. This will become more critical in the future the time and space separating the two phases condenses.

The sixth area for consideration is the role of civil affairs and the role of the common soldier. Many of the documents addressed in this monograph point to civil affairs soldiers as the responsible party for an occupation. This is important as they hold the expertise and training in all the stability and support tasks. As such, it is important to integrate them into combat arms team. However, the civil affairs soldier cannot do everything, as the common soldier in infantry and artillery battalions need to perform these missions as readily as a civil affairs soldier.

The seventh area is the importance of the interagency team. In all three cases, the development of the interagency team could have been better. In Germany, the State Department struggled with the Secretary of War for control in Germany. The case was the same in Iraq as Colonel Kevin Benson, C-5 CFLCC, OIF, has repeatedly stated the difficulties in working with other government agencies.[189] In Panama, the struggle for a correct operational tempo and synergy with the other government agencies was at issue. This is not just a problem with an occupation, it occurs at all levels of war and all missions. It needs to be fixed in order to fully implement the United States' instruments of power.

The eighth area for consideration, another principle of war, is economy of force. The definition of economy of force is to "allocate minimum essential combat power to secondary efforts."[190] In an occupation economy of force additionally means taking appropriate risk in employing forces across the occupied territory. As an example in Germany, a Constabulary force was established to better distribute manpower. However, the insurgency movement in Iraq poses an unacceptable risk with such a distribution.

---

[189] Author's notes taken from SAMS lecture on Operation Iraqi Freedom, December 2003, Fort. Leavenworth, KS.

[190] *FM 3.0*, 4-13.

The last area for consideration is that of financial procedures for the occupation forces. As Major General Petraeus stated, "money is ammunition."[191] The Commander's Emergency Response Program is one method that has worked in Iraq. Not only does the injection of money fix the problems it was aimed at, it also creates jobs and infuses the economy with money. Measures should be taken to ensure that money is expedited to the places where it can do the most good. Planning for these activities should be included in future occupations.

This monograph has offered a model to examine and plan future occupations. It has distilled the law and case studies into essential tasks and considerations that could form the basis of occupation doctrine. It has also pointed out that occupation doctrine does not currently exist. This is a void that needs to be filled. The United States has an unprecedented position of power in world and has been the target of terrorism. As such the United States has stated its intent to protect itself to ensure its safety. The current chaotic state of world affairs will continue and the possibility of the United States removing rogue governments and reestablishing nations is high. The United States Army must take the lead again as it did prior to World War II and create doctrine that will aide in the highly probable future occupations.

---

[191] Gordon, 8.

WORKS CITED

Backer, John. "From Morgenthau Plan to Marshall Plan." *Americans as Proconsuls: United States Military Government in Germany and Japan, 1944-1952.* Carbondale, IL: Southern Illinois University Press, 1984.

Banusiewicz, John D. " Bremer: 'Future of Hope' in Iraq includes Justice." *Armed Forces Information Service.* 14 November 2003.
<http://www.defenselink.mil/news/Nov2003/n11142003_200311147.html> [12 JAN 2004].

Bearak, Barry. "Unreconstructed." *New York Times.* 1 June 2003.

Benvenisti, Eyal. *The International Law of Occupation.* Princeton: Princeton University Press, 1993.

Bowers, Paul. "Iraq: law of occupation." Research Paper, House of Commons Library, Research Paper 03/51, London, 2 June 2003.

Building Justice. < http://www.cpa-iraq.org/security/justice.html> [12 Jan 2004].

Burns, John F. "Threats and Responses: The Great Escapes; Hussein and Mobs Virtually Empty Iraq's Prisons." New York Times, 21 October 2002.

"Bush Reassures Turkey on Kurds." Washingtontimes.com. 28 Jan 2004.
<http://washingtontimes.com/upi-breaking/20040128-033953-6801r.htm> [28 Jan 2004]

Center for Strategic and International Studies (CSIS) and Association of the United States Army. "Post-Conflict Reconstruction Task Framework." May 2002.

Coalition Provisional Authority, *Regulation Number 1*, Section 1, (Baghdad, Iraq: 16 May 2003),
<http://www.cpa-iraq.org/regulations/REG1.pdf> [12 January 2004].

Cole, Ronald H. *Operation JUST CAUSE: The Planning and Execution of Joint Operations in Panama, February 1988–January 1990.* Washington, D.C. Joint History Office, Office of the Chairman of the Joint Chiefs of Staff. 1995.

Cordesman, Anthony H. "Developments in Iraq at the end of 2003: Adapting US Policy to Stay the Course." Center for Strategic and International Studies. Revised 30 December 2003.
<http://csis.org/features/iraq.cfm> [12 JAN 2004]

———. "Iraq: Too Uncertain To Call." Center for Strategic and International Studies. 14 November 2003. < http://csis.org/features/iraq.cfm> [12 JAN 2004]

———. "The 'War After the War' In Iraq; Evolving Conflict, possible Scenarios, and the Data and Analytic Tools Needed to Understand What is Happening." Center for Strategic and International Studies. 8 August 2003. <http://csis.org/features/iraq.cfm> [12 JAN 2004]

———. "The Current Military Situation in Iraq." Center for Strategic and International Studies. 14 November 2003. < http://csis.org/features/iraq.cfm> [12 JAN 2004]

———. "What is Next in Iraq? Military Developments, Military Requirements and Armed Nation Building." Center for Strategic and International Studies. 21 August 2003. < http://csis.org/features/iraq.cfm> [12 JAN 2004]

Crane, Conrad C and W. Andrew Terrill. "Reconstruction Iraq: Insights Challenges, and Mission for Military Forces in a Post-Conflict Scenario." Monograph, Strategic Studies Institute, U.S. Army War College, Carlisle, PA, 2003.

Department of Defense. *Joint Publication 1-02, Dictionary for Military and Associated Terms.* Headquarters, Joint Chiefs of Staff. 17 December 2003. <http://www.dtic.mil/doctrine/jel/new_pubs/jp1_02.pdf> [24 JAN 2004]

———. *Joint Publication 3-0, Doctrine for Joint Operations.* Headquarters, Joint Chiefs of Staff. Washington D.C. 10 September 2001.

———. *Joint Publication 3-57, Joint Doctrine for Civil-Military Operations.* Headquarters, Joint Chiefs of Staff. Washington D.C. 8 Feb 2001.

———. *Joint Publication 3-57.1, Joint Doctrine for Civil Affairs.* Headquarters, Joint Chiefs of Staff. Washington D.C. 14 April 2003.

———. *JP 3-07, Joint Doctrine for Military Operations Other than War.* Headquarters, Joint Chiefs of Staff. 16 June 1995.

Department of the Army. *Department of the Army Pamphlet, 27-1 Treaties Governing Land Warfare.* Washington, D.C.: Headquarters, Department of the Army, 1956.

———. *Field Manual 27-10, The Law of Land Warfare.* Washington, D.C.: Headquarters, Department of the Army, 1956.

———. *Field Manual 41-10, Civil Affairs Operations.* Washington, D.C.: Headquarters, Department of the Army, 1993.

———. *Field Manual 41-10, Civil Affairs Operations.* Washington, D.C.: Department of the Army, 2000.

———. *FM 3-0, Operations.* Washington, D.C.: Headquarters, Department of the Army, 2001.

———. *FM 3-07, Stability Operations and Support Operations.* Washington, D.C.: Headquarters, Department of the Army, 2003.

Departments of the Army and Navy. *Field Manual 27-5, OPNAV 50E-3, Military Government and Civil Affairs.* Washington, D.C.: Headquarters, Departments of the Army and Navy, 1943.

———. *Field Manual 27-5, OPNAV P22-1115, Civil Affairs Military Government.* Washington, D.C.: Headquarters, Departments of the Army and Navy, 1947.

Dobbins, James and John G. McGinn, Keith Crane, Seth G. Jones, Rollie Lal, Andrew Rathmell, Rachel Swanger, Anga Timilsina. *America's Role In Nation Building: From Germany to Iraq.* Santa Monica, CA: Rand, 2003.

Doty, Grant R. "The United States and the Development of the Laws of Land Warfare." *Military Law Review* 156 (June 1998): 224-255.

Economy. <http://www.cpa-iraq.org/economy.html> [12 JAN 2004].

England, Andrew. "Explosion rocks Jordanian Embassy in Iraq, kills at least 11." *Seattle Times*, 8 August 2003. <http://seattletimes.nwsource.com/html/nationworld/2001406000 _webiraqexplosion07.html> [12 Jan 2004].

Fallows, James. "Blind into Baghdad." *The Atlantic Monthly*, January/February, 2004, 53-74.

Fastabend, David. "The Categorization of Conflict." *Parameters* XXVII, no. 2 (Summer 1997): 75-87.

Fishel, John T. *The Fog of Peace: Planning and Executing the Restoration of Panama*. Carlisle Barracks, PA: Strategic Studies Institute, U.S. Army War College, 1992.

————. *Civil Military Operations in the New World*. Westport, Connecticut: Praeger, 1997.

————. and Richard D. Downie. "Taking Responsibility for our Actions? Establishing Order and Stability in Panama." *Military Review* (April 1992): 66-77.

Flanagan, E.M. "The Occupation of Japan." *Army*, August, 1995, 48-52.

Friedman, Thomas L. *The Lexus and the Olive Tree*. New York: Anchor Books, 2000.

Geneva Convention Relative to the Protection of Civilian Persons in Time of War, 12 August 1949.

Gilmore, Gerry J. "'Incredible Progress' Made Restoring Iraq's Infrastructure, Officials Say." *American Forces Information Service*. 7 July 2003. <www.defenselink.mil/news/july2003/> [12 JAN 2004].

Gimbel, John. *The American Occupation of Germany, Politics and the Military, 1945-1949*. Stanford: Stanford University Press, 1968.

Gordon, Michael R. "101st Airborne Scores Success in Northern Iraq." *New York Times*, 4 Sept 2003.

Graber, Doris A. *The Development of the Law of Belligerent Occupation 1863-1914*. New York: Columbia University Press, 1949.

Greenspan, Morris. *The Modern Law of Land Warfare*. Berkeley, CA: University of California Press, 1959.

Grimmett, Richard F. "Instances of Use of United States Armed Forces Abroad, 1798-1999." Research paper RL30172, The Library of Congress, Congressional Research Service, Washington, D.C, Updated 17 May 1999.

Hague Convention No. IV Respecting the Laws and Customs of War on Land. 18 October 1907.

Hawk, Jeff. "Water Flows from the Desert." *USMC News*. 15 April 2003. <http://www.globalsecurity.org/wmd/library/news/iraq/2003/iraq-030415-usmc01.htm> [12 JAN 2004].

Hudson, Walter M. "The U.S. Military Government and Democratic Reform and Denazification in Bavaria, 1945-47." Master's thesis, U.S. Army Command and General Staff College, Fort Leavenworth, KS, 2001.

Ignatieff, Michael. "Why Are We in Iraq?" *New York Times Magazine*. 7 September 2003.

Iraq Council Members Meet With U.N. Fox News Channel, July 22, 2003. <http://www.foxnews.com/story/0,2933,92589,00.html. [24 JAN 2004].

Iraq Reconstruction. <http://www.globalsecurity.org/military/ops/iraq_recon_intro/> [12 JAN 2004].

Iraqi Military Reconstruction." <http://www.globalsecurity.org/military/world/iraq/iraq-corps.htm> [12 JAN 2004].

Johnston, David. "The Struggle for Iraq: Evidence; Plenty of Clues in Iraqi Crimes, but few Trials." *New York Times*. 23 September 2003.

Joint Chief of Staff. "Directive to Commander-in-Chief of United States Forces of Occupation Regarding the Military Government of Germany (JCS1067)." April 1945. <http://www.usembassy.de/usa/etexts/ga3-450426.pdf> [12 JAN 2004].

Joint Staff/Coalition Provisional Authority. Iraq Weekly Update. 09 Jan 2004. <http://www.globalsecurity.org/ wmd/library/news/iraq/2004/01/iraq-weekly-js-cpa-20040109.pdf> [12 JAN 2004].

Kifner, John. "Remaking History: Britain Tried First. It Was No Picnic Then." *New York Times*. 20 July 2003

Martins, Mark. "No Small Change of Soldiering: The Commander's Emergency Response Program (CERP) in Iraq and Afghanistan." *Army Lawyer*, (February, 2004): 1-20.

McCreedy, Kenneth O. "Planning the peace: Operation Eclipse and the Occupation of Germany." Monograph., School of Advanced Military Studies, United States Army Command and General Staff College, Fort Leavenworth, KS, 1995.

————. "Winning the Peace: Postconflict Operations." Monograph, School of Advanced Military Studies, United States Army Command and General Staff College, Fort Leavenworth, KS, 1994.

Menk, Peter D. "Post-Conflict Strategic Requirements Workshop." *Center for Strategic Leadership, Issue Paper 1-01*, January, 2001.

Michael Bernhard. "The Lessons of Successful Military Occupation." *Strategic Insights 2*. No.5. May 2003.

"President Bush Discusses Freedom in Iraq and Middle East." Remarks by the President at the 20th Anniversary of the National Endowment for Democracy, United States Chamber of Commerce. Washington, D.C. 6 November 2003. <http://www.whitehouse.gov/news/releases/2003/11/20031106-2.html> [12 Jan 2004].

Recknegel, Charles. "Iraq: Oil Production Strengthens but Remains Problematic." Radio Free Europe/Radio Liberty. 31 July 2003. <http://www.globalsecurity.org/wmd/library/news/iraq/2003/07/iraq-030731-rfel-151445.htm> [24 Jan 2004].

Religious Structures. <http://www.globalsecurity.org/military/world/iraq/religion.htm> [12 Jan 2004]

Representative Government at the local level." <http://www.cpa-iraq.org/government/local_level.html> [12 JAN 2004].

Rivkin, David B. Jr. and Darin R. Bartram. "Military Occupation: Legally ensuring a Lasting Peace." *The Washington Quarterly* 26 (Summer 2003): 87-103.

Rubin, Alissa J. "U.S. Struggles in Quicksand of Iraq." *Los Angeles Times*, May 5 2003.

Sachs, Susan. "A Region Inflamed: Occupation; Baathists, Once Reviled, Prove Difficult to Remove." *New York Times.* November 21 2003.

————. "A Region Inflamed: Occupation; Baathists, Once Reviled, Prove Difficult to Remove." *New York Times*. 21 November 2003.

————. "The Struggle for Iraq: Toward a Trial; The prosecution of a Dictator; A Decade's Digging is Already Done." *New York Times*. 17 December 2003.

Schmitt, Eric. "The Struggle for Iraq: Rebuilding; G.I.'s Provide Public works as Well as Security to Iraqis." *New York Times*. 30 December 2003.

————. "The Struggle for Iraq: The Occupation; Iraqi and Soldiers try to adjust to Unfamiliar Roles." *New York Times*. 18 December 2003.

Slater, Eric and Laura King. "Court Back in Session in Baghdad." *L.A. Times*. 9 May 2003.

Spinner, Jackie. "Iraqi Oil Gets Its Own Police Force." *Washington Post.* 17 January 2004. <http://www.washingtonpost.com/ac2/wp-dyn/A23664-2004Jan16> [24 Jan 2004].

Supreme Headquarters Allied Expeditionary Force. *Handbook for Military Government in Germany*. 1944. <http://www-cgsc.army.mil/carl/resources/books.asp#military> [12 JAN 2004].

Svitak, Amy and Alex Neill. "Iraq divided into 3 Zones to ease postwar efforts." Air Force Times. 5 May 2003.

Telecoms. <http://www.cpa-iraq.org/essential_services/telecoms.html> [12 JAN 2004].

Trowbridge, Gordon. "'I hope these are not just words' Civil Affairs team tries to deliver promises to Iraqis." *Army Times*. 19 May 2003.

United Nations Statistical database. <http://millenniumindicators.un.org/unsd/mi/mi_goals.asp> [12 Feb 2004].

United States Central Command. "120 Baathists Renounce Political Party." *CENTCOM News Release.* 20 January 2004, Release Number 04-01-50. <http://www.centcom.mil/CENTCOMNews/release_list.asp> [23 JAN 2004]

————. "Conference Seeks Ways to Improve Iraq's Water Supply." *CENTOCOM News Release.* 21 January 2004, Release Number 04-01-52. <http://www.centcom.mil/CENTCOMNews/release_list.asp> [23 JAN 2004].

————. "Conference Seeks Ways to Improve Iraq's Water Supply." *News Release*, January 21 2004, sec. Release Number 04-01-52, .

Von Glahn, Gerhard. *The Occupation of Enemy Territory*. Minneapolis: The University of Minnesota Press, 1957.

Water Resources. <http://www.cpa-iraq.org/essential_services/water-management.html> [12 JAN 2004].

Weisman, Steven R. "A Foreign Policy of Try, Try Again." *New York Times*. 18 January 2003.

A Wiser Peace: An Action Strategy for a Post-Conflict Iraq. By Frederick D. Barton and Bathsheba N. Crocker, Project Directors. Washington, D.C.: Center for Strategic and International Studies, 2003.

Wollschlaeger, Daria, LTC. *Post-Conflict Governance*. Charlottesville, VA: The United States Army Judge Advocate General School, 2003. PowerPoint Presentation.

Woodward, Bob. *The Commanders*. New York: Simon & Schuster, 1991.

Ziemke, Earl F. *The U.S. Army in the Occupation of Germany 1944-1946*. Washington, D.C.: Center of Military History United States Army, 1975.

Zink, Harold. *American Military Government in Germany*. New York: Macmillan, 1947.